Samuel French Acting Edition

A Christmas Survival Guide

A Miniature Christmas Spectacular!

Created and Written by
James Hindman &
Ray Roderick

Music Arrangements by
John Glaudini

SAMUELFRENCH.COM   SAMUELFRENCH.CO.UK

Book and Lyrics Copyright © 2003 by
James Hindman, Ray Roderick, and John Glaudini
All Rights Reserved

A CHRISTMAS SURVIVAL GUIDE is fully protected under the copyright laws of the United States of America, the British Commonwealth, including Canada, and all other countries of the Copyright Union. All rights, including professional and amateur stage productions, recitation, lecturing, public reading, motion picture, radio broadcasting, television and the rights of translation into foreign languages are strictly reserved.

ISBN 978-0-573-62980-8

www.SamuelFrench.com
www.SamuelFrench.co.uk

For Production Enquiries

United States and Canada
Info@SamuelFrench.com
1-866-598-8449

United Kingdom and Europe
Plays@SamuelFrench.co.uk
020-7255-4302

Each title is subject to availability from Samuel French, depending upon country of performance. Please be aware that *A CHRISTMAS SURVIVAL GUIDE* may not be licensed by Samuel French in your territory. Professional and amateur producers should contact the nearest Samuel French office or licensing partner to verify availability.

CAUTION: Professional and amateur producers are hereby warned that *A CHRISTMAS SURVIVAL GUIDE* is subject to a licensing fee. Publication of this play(s) does not imply availability for performance. Both amateurs and professionals considering a production are strongly advised to apply to Samuel French before starting rehearsals, advertising, or booking a theatre. A licensing fee must be paid whether the title(s) is presented for charity or gain and whether or not admission is charged. Professional/Stock licensing fees are quoted upon application to Samuel French.

No one shall make any changes in this title(s) for the purpose of production. No part of this book may be reproduced, stored in a retrieval system, or transmitted in any form, by any means, now known or yet to be invented, including mechanical, electronic, photocopying, recording, videotaping, or otherwise, without the prior written permission of the publisher. No one shall upload this title(s), or part of this title(s), to any social media websites.

For all enquiries regarding motion picture, television, and other media rights, please contact Samuel French.

MUSIC USE NOTE

Licensees are solely responsible for obtaining formal written permission from copyright owners to use copyrighted music in the performance of this play and are strongly cautioned to do so. If no such permission is obtained by the licensee, then the licensee must use only original music that the licensee owns and controls. Licensees are solely responsible and liable for all music clearances and shall indemnify the copyright owners of the play(s) and their licensing agent, Samuel French, against any costs, expenses, losses and liabilities arising from the use of music by licensees. Please contact the appropriate music licensing authority in your territory for the rights to any incidental music.

IMPORTANT BILLING AND CREDIT REQUIREMENTS

If you have obtained performance rights to this title, please refer to your licensing agreement for important billing and credit requirements.

"(Everybody's Waitin' for) The Man with the Bag" by Irving Taylor, Dudley Brooks, Hal Stanley. © 1954 (Renewed) Morley Music Co. All rights reserved. Used by permission.

"All Those Christmas Clichés" Lyrics by Lynn Ahrens, Music by Steve Flaherty. © 1993 WB Music Corp. All rights on behalf of Pen and Perseverance (ASCAP) & Hillsdale Music, Inc. (ASCAP) administered by WB Music Corp. (ASCAP) All rights reserved. Used by permission.

"Silver Bells" by Jay Livingston and Ray Evans. © 1952 (Renewed) Published by Paramount Music Corp. All rights reserved. Used by permission.

"This Will Be the Best Christmas Ever!" Music by John Glaudini, Lyrics by Bernie Garzia. © 2002 by authors. Used by permission. All rights reserved.

"I'd Like to Hitch a Ride with Santa Claus" By Johnny Burke and Jimmy Van Heusen. Published by Famous Music Corp. Used by permission. All rights reserved.

"The Happy New Year Blues" Music and Lyrics by Irving Berlin. This selection is used by special arrangement with The Rodgers and Hammerstein Organization, 1065 Avenue of the Americas, Suite 2400, New York, New York 10018.

"Reindeer Boogie" By Hank Snow, Charlie Faircloth, Cordia Volkmar. © 1953 by authors. This song is used with special permission of Ernest Tubb Music. All rights reserved.

"Christmas Eve" Words and Music by Julie Gold. © 2002 Cherry River Music Co. (BMI)/Julie Gold Music (BMI). Worldwide rights for Julie Gold Music administered by Cherry River Music Co. (BMI). All rights reserved. Used by permission.

"Santa Fantasy" and "The Greatest Gift" Lyrics by Cheryl Stern, Music by John Glaudini. © 2003 by John Glaudini and Fearless Leider. Used by special permission of Fearless Leider. All rights reserved.

"Surabaya—Santa" (from Songs for a New World) Music and Lyrics by Jason Robert Brown, additional text by Kristine Zbornik. © 1996 Jason Robert Brown. All rights controlled by Semolina Farfalle Music Co. Inc. (ASCAP)

"Santa Claus Is Back in Town" Written by Jerry Leiber and Mike Stoller. © 1957. Used by permission of Jerry Leiber Music and Mike Stoller Music. All rights reserved.

"Rudolph the Red Nosed Reindeer," A Holly Jolly Christmas," Silver and Gold" and "The Most Wonderful Day of the Year" Music and Lyrics by Johnny Marks. © 1960 by St. Nicholas Music. Used by special permission. All rights reserved.

"Frosty the Snowman" By Steve Nelson and Jack Rollins. © 1950 (Renewed) Chappell & Co. (ASCAP). All rights reserved. Used by permission.

"Put One Foot in Front of the Other" By Jules Bass and Maury Laws. © 1970 (Renewed) Lorimar Music Corp (ASCAP). All rights on behalf of Lorimar Music Corp. (ASCAP) administered by WB Music Corp. (ASCAP). All rights reserved. Used by permission.

"Feliz Navidad" By Jose Feliciano. © 1970 Jose Feliciano. Used with permission by J & H Publishing from Stollman & Grubman, PA. 2424 North Federal Highway, Suite 450, Boca Raton, FL 33431. All rights reserved. Used by permission.

"The Christmas Song" By Mel Torme and Robert Wells. © 1946 Edwin Morris & Company, a division of MPL Communications, Inc. All rights reserved. Used by permission.

"Little Girl Blue" Music by Richard Rodgers, Lyrics by Lorenz Hart. This selection is used by special arrangement with The Rodgers and Hammerstein Organization, 1065 Avenue of the Americas, Suite 2400, New York, New York 10018.

"Some Children" By Wihla Hutson and Alfred Bart. © 1954 by authors. Used with special permission by Hollis Music, NY. The Richmond Organization, 11 West 19th Street, New York, New York 10011. All rights reserved. Used by permission.

A CHRISTMAS SURVIVAL GUIDE

was first produced at
Arci's Place in New York City

with the following cast:

MAN	Brian Sutherland
WOMAN 1	Karyn Quackenbush
WOMAN 2	Kerry O'Malley

Directed by
Ray Roderick

The first production of

A CHRISTMAS SURVIVAL GUIDE

with a cast of five was produced at
Westchester Broadway Theatre

with the following cast:

MAN 1	Brian Sutherland
MAN 2	Jim Price
WOMAN 1	Diane Sutherland
WOMAN 2	Kaitlin Hopkins
WOMAN 3	Gina Valentine

Directed by
Keith Cromwell

CASTING NOTE

A Christmas Survival Guide requires likable and versatile performers with strong vocal ability and a comedic flair. The script indicates roles for five performers.

If desired, the show can be performed with a cast of three. Refer to appendixes A and B on pages 71 — 83 for details on role assignments and specific revisions for the smaller cast.

MUSICAL NUMBERS FOR CAST OF 5

ACT I

Carol of the Bells	ALL
Everybody's Waitin' for the Man with the Bag	ALL
We Wish You a Merry Christmas	ALL
All Those Christmas Clichés	WOMAN 1
Silver Bells	MAN 1
This Will Be the Best Christmas Ever	WOMAN 2 & MAN 2
The Christmas Party / I'd Like to Hitch a Ride with Santa Claus	
	WOMAN 3
The Happy New Year Blues	ALL
Reindeer Boogie / Jingle Bells	PIANO PLAYER, ALL
Christmas Eve	WOMAN 2
Santa Fantasy	MAN 2
Silent Night	INSTRUMENTAL
Surabaya Santa	WOMAN 3
Santa Claus Is Back in Town	MAN 1 & WOMEN

ACT II

The Twelve Steps of Christmas	WOMAN 2
TV Christmas Medley	WOMEN 1 & 3 & MAN 2
Rudolph the Red Nosed Reindeer	
A Holly Jolly Christmas	
Silver and Gold	
Frosty the Snowman	
Put One Foot in Front of the Other	
Feliz Navidad	
The Christmas Song	
Hark the Herald Angels Sing	
Little Girl Blue	WOMAN 3
An Old-Fashioned Sleigh Ride	MAN 1 & WOMEN 2 & 3
Sacred Trio	MAN 1 & ALL WOMEN
Away in a Manger	
Some Children See Him	
Amazing Grace	
O Holy Night	MAN 2, ALL
The Greatest Gift	ALL
Everybody's Waitin' for the Man with the Bag	ALL

Special Thanks

*Bob Funking, Bill Stutler, Lisa Tiso, everyone at
Westchester Broadway Theatre, Tom Stajmiger,
Stepping Out Productions, Maria Glaudini, John Ploetz,
Karyn Quackenbush, Siobhan O'Neill, Dana Kenn,
American Graphics, Mark Sendroff and Associates,
Eric Goldman, Wayne Schroder, Alice Cohen, Julie Gold,
Cheryl Stern, Barbara Tirrell, Peter Ligeti, Jason Brantman,
Mike Grainey, everyone at City Stage, Luis Torregrosa,
James Marino, Caralyn Spector, Eric Haugen
and our friends and family.*

ACT I

(Christmas decorations adorn the theater. The five-piece band sits onstage. The pianist is furthest DS in front of the other members of the band who sit on a raised platform disguised as a mound of snow. Behind them is a row of lighted Christmas trees, an urban skyline and lighted cyc. The set is reminiscent of Christmas television specials we know and love. Somewhere on the set is a large blow up of our book, "A Christmas Survival Guide."
The lights fade to black except on the book. SFX: phone ring...another ring...the click of the answering machine.)

BOOK (MALE VOICEOVER). Hello, you've reached the office of Doctor Ted, Ph.D. in psychology. I'm either on another line or sunbathing in Acapulco, so please leave a message after the beep. I also urge you to pick up my new, best-selling book, "A Christmas Survival Guide." Designed to help you embrace the true meaning of the holiday season, and keep you from getting bogged down in all that merchandising and commercialism. And for only $34.95 plus tax, it makes the perfect stocking stuffer! So look for it today, "A Christmas Survival Guide! – and don't forget to wait for the beep!

(Piano: bell tone. The lights go down on the book.)

FEMALE VOICEOVER. Attention shoppers! There are now only 174 shopping days left 'til Christmas. Happy Fourth of July!

(Offstage voices begin singing in sweet a cappella as the lights on stage and around the theater slowly change. Our FEMALE VOICEOVER continues.)

CAROL OF THE BELLS

WOMAN 2.
HARK, HOW THE BELLS
SWEET SILVER BELLS
ALL SEEM TO SAY
"THROW CARES AWAY"

VOICEOVER. Only 127 shopping days left.

(The countdown continues as this cacophony builds, becoming more and more chaotic.)

WOMAN 2 & MAN 1.
CHRISTMAS IS HERE
BRINGING GOOD CHEER
TO YOUNG AND OLD
MEEK AND THE BOLD.

WOMEN 1 & 3 & MAN 2.
DING, DONG, DING, DONG
THAT IS THEIR SONG
WITH JOYFUL RING
ALL CAROLING

VOICEOVER. 73 days left!

WOMEN 1 & 2 & MAN 1.
ONE SEEMS TO HEAR
WORDS OF GOOD CHEER
FROM EVERY WHERE
FILLING THE AIR

WOMAN 3 & MAN 2.
DING DONG IN
FORTY-TWO MORE DAYS.
VOICEOVER. 42 days.

MAN 2 & WOMEN 2 & 3.
O, HOW THEY POUND
RAISING THE SOUND
O'ER HILL AND DALE
TELLING THEIR TALE

WOMAN 1 & MAN 1.
DING DONG IN
THIRTY-THREE MORE DAYS
VOICEOVER. Thirty-three.

MEN 1 & 2 & WOMEN 1 & 2.
GAILY THEY RING
WHILE PEOPLE SING
WORDS OF GOOD CHEER
CHRISTMAS IS HERE!

WOMAN 3.
TWENTY-SEVEN MORE DAYS
VOICEOVER. Twenty-seven.
GOD I HATE THIS SONG

WOMEN.
MERRY MERRY MERRY
CHRISTMAS

MEN.
IN FIVE DAYS
VOICEOVER. Five!

MAN 1 & WOMAN 2.
MERRY MERRY MERRY
MERRY CHRISTMAS

WOMAN 2 AND MAN 2.
FOUR DAYS
VOICEOVER. Four!

MAN 2 & WOMAN 2.
MERRY MERRY MERRY
MERRY MERRY MERRY
   ALL.
CHRISTMAS IS HERE!
CHRISTMAS IS HERE!
CHRISTMAS IS HERE!
CHRISTMAS IS …
	WOMAN 1 & MAN 1.
	THREE DAYS
	   VOICEOVER. Three!
	
	   VOICEOVER. Happy Thanksgiving.

(The song and sounds abruptly stop. One by one the five ACTORS enter reading their books.)

   BOOK (VOICEOVER). Dear Reader,
Perhaps you've picked up this book because you'd like to enjoy this holiday season but, like many, you find it too disappointing, too stressful, too lonely, too scary. Believe me, you're not alone. *(All turning page.)* This cherished time of year can turn even the cheeriest of folk toward dark and moody thoughts. Well, fear no more. Armed with this book and an optimistic attitude, you're bound to have your best holiday season ever!

WAITING FOR THE MAN WITH THE BAG

   WOMAN 2.
OLD MR. KRINGLE
IS SOON GONNA JINGLE
THE BELLS THAT'LL TINGLE ALL YOUR TROUBLES AWAY
EVERYBODY'S WAITIN' FOR THE MAN WITH THE BAG
'CAUSE CHRISTMAS IS COMIN' AGAIN

   MAN 1.
HE'S GOT A SLEIGH FULL
IT'S NOT GONNA STAY FULL
   WOMAN 1.
HE'S GOT STUFF TO DROP AT EVERY STOP OF THE WAY
   MAN 1 & WOMAN 1.
EVERYBODY'S WAITIN' FOR THE MAN WITH THE BAG
   MAN 1 & WOMEN 1 & 2.
'CAUSE CHRISTMAS IS COMIN' AGAIN

MAN 2.
HE'LL BE HERE
WITH THE ANSWERS TO THE PRAYERS
THAT YOU'VE MADE THROUGH THE YEAR
    WOMAN 3.
YOU'LL GET YOURS
IF YOU'VE DONE EVERYTHING YOU SHOULD
    MAN 2.
BEEN EXTRA SPECIAL GOOD
    WOMAN 1.
HE'LL MAKE THIS DECEMBER
    MAN 1 & WOMEN 1 & 2.
THE ONE YOU'LL REMEMBER

(They form a clump center stage.)

    ALL.
THE BEST AND THE MERRIEST YOU EVER DID HAVE
EVERYBODY'S WAITIN' FOR THE MAN WITH THE BAG
CHRISTMAS IS HERE AGAIN

    ALL. *(During voiceover.)*
FA, LA LA LA. FA, LA LA LA ...

    BOOK (VOICEOVER). Still reading? Proof positive— significant change is even closer than you think. Feel your personal holiday spirit beginning to come alive? *(ACTORS nod yes.)* Feel the tingle? *(They do.)* I bet you can! With a little practice and some well-placed mistletoe, this holiday season will find you skating with the best of them!

    ALL. *(Looking up from their books.)*
FA LA LA, HAPPY HOLIDAY!

OLD MR. KRINGLE
IS SOON GONNA JINGLE
ALL THE BELLS THAT'LL TINGLE ALL YOUR TROUBLES
    AWAY
EVERYBODY'S WAITIN' FOR THE MAN WITH THE BAG
CHRISTMAS IS HERE AGAIN

WOMEN.
HE'LL BE HERE

WITH THE ANSWER TO THE
PRAYERS
THAT YOU'VE MADE
THROUGH THE YEAR
   MEN.
YOU'LL GET YOURS

IF YOU'VE DONE EVERYTHING
YOU SHOULD
   WOMEN 2 & 3.
BEEN EXTRA SPECIAL GOOD
   WOMAN 1.
JUST LIKE I KNEW YOU WOULD

   ALL.
HE'LL MAKE THIS DECEMBER
THE ONE TO REMEMBER
THE BEST AND THE MERRIEST
YOU EVER DID HAVE
EVERYBODY'S WAITIN'

THEY'RE ALL CONGREGATIN'
WAITIN' FOR THE MAN
   WOMAN 1.
WITH THE BAG

   ALL.
YOU BETTER WATCH OUT NOW!

   MEN.
HE'LL BE HERE

OOO ...

   WOMEN.
YOU'LL GET YOURS

   MAN 1.
EVERYBODY

   WOMEN 2 & 3 & MEN.
WITH THE BAG

(They end reading from their books. MAN 2 and WOMAN 2 sing their way off stage right. MAN 1 and WOMAN 3 exit arm in arm stage left.)

WE WISH YOU A MERRY CHRISTMAS
   ALL.
WE WISH YOU A MERRY CHRISTMAS
WE WISH YOU A MERRY CHRISTMAS

WE WISH YOU A MERRY CHRISTMAS
AND A HAPPY NEW YEAR.

WOMAN 1.	**MEN & WOMEN 2 & 3.**
WE WISH YOU A MERRY CHRISTMAS	BA DA BA DA ...
AND A HAPPY NEW YEAR	

(WOMAN 1 is left alone on stage. She sets her book on the piano and sings.)

ALL THOSE CHRISTMAS CLICHÉS

WOMAN 1.
I'VE SPENT CHRISTMAS IN PEORIA
CHRISTMAS IN SCHENECTADY
CHRISTMAS IN LAS VEGAS AND LA
AND I ALWAYS THOUGHT
IT COULDN'T MATTER LESS
BUT LATELY COME DECEMBER
I CONFESS

I WANT THE TREE FULL OF TOYS AND TINSEL
I WANT THE WREATH ON THE RED FRONT DOOR
I WANT THE ELVES IN THE YARD
AND EACH SENTIMENTAL CARD
DRIPPING GLITTER ON THE FLOOR

I WANT A ROOF FULL OF PLYWOOD REINDEER
I WANT A ROAD FULL OF HORSE DRAWN SLEIGHS
ALL THOSE CHRISTMAS CLICHÉS

(She crosses down stage left.)

I WANT THE TURKEY WITH ALL THE TRIMMINGS
THE TURKEY MOM HARDLY EVER MADE
I WANT THE GULP AND THE TEAR
AT THE MOMENT THAT I HEAR
JOHNNY MATHIS BEING PLAYED

I WANT A LAKE FULL OF PERFECT SKATERS
I WANT THAT FRUITCAKE WITH SUGAR GLAZE
ALL THOSE CHRISTMAS CLICHÉS

NOT TO MENTION THE SNOW
NOT TO MENTION THE CHOIR
NOT TO MENTION THE CANDLES IN THE WINDOW
AND CHESTNUTS ROASTING ON THE FIRE

INSIDE A HOUSE FILLED WITH NOISE AND LAUGHTER
ALONG A STREET PAVED IN TWINKLING LIGHT
I WANT THE BELLS AND THE DRUMS
MISTLETOE AND SUGAR PLUMS
AND KIDS TO TUCK IN TIGHT

(She crosses up stage center, then turns front.)

AND AS FOR THE GUY IN THE BRIGHT RED OUTFIT
INSTEAD OF FLYING OFF, HE STAYS.
ALL THOSE CHRISTMAS CLICHÉS
I WANT THOSE OVERUSED, CORNY,
ENDLESSLY LOVELY CHRISTMAS CLICHÉS.

(Lovely church bells and chimes fill the air. WOMAN 1 watches a happy couple in love, WOMAN 2 and MAN 2, cross the stage carrying a Christmas tree they are taking home to decorate.
MAN 1 enters and watches the couple as well. He gives WOMAN 1 a knowing look. WOMAN 1 exits. MAN 1 is left on stage. He starts out the song very sweetly with a sense of calm. But as the song continues, he becomes overwhelmed by the sounds and chaos of the season. Comic and Chaplin-like, he mimes the world coming at him.)

SILVER BELLS

MAN 1.
CHRISTMAS MAKES YOU FEEL EMOTIONAL
IT MAY BRING PARTIES OR THOUGHTS DEVOTIONAL
WHATEVER HAPPENS OR WHAT MAY BE
HERE IS WHAT CHRISTMAS TIME MEANS TO ME

CITY SIDEWALKS, BUSY SIDEWALKS
DRESSED IN HOLIDAY STYLE
IN THE AIR THERE'S A FEELING OF CHRISTMAS

CHILDREN LAUGHING, PEOPLE PASSING
MEETING SMILE AFTER SMILE
AND ON EV'RY STREET CORNER YOU HEAR

(A cell phone rings. MAN stops, looks around the audience to find the idiot who forgot to turn theirs off, realizes it's his own, and answers it.) Hello. Yeah, I'm kind of in the middle of something right now. Yeah, I'll be there. *(He closes his phone and picks up where he left off.)*

SILVER BELLS, SILVER BELLS
IT'S CHRISTMAS TIME IN THE CITY.

(MAN's watch buzzer goes off. He turns it off.)

RING A LING, HEAR THEM RING
SOON IT WILL BE CHRISTMAS DAY.

(Another phone rings. PIANO PLAYER hands MAN a phone. He answers it.) Hello. Yes, I said I'll be there. Yeah, fine. *(MAN puts on his hat and walks downstage as if he is going outside.)*

STRINGS OF STREET LIGHTS
(Car horn.)
EVEN STOP LIGHTS,
(Car horn.)
BLINK A BRIGHT RED AND GREEN.
(Truck horn.)
AS THE SHOPPERS RUSH HOME WITH THEIR TREASURES.
(Sound of a boom-box going by.)
HEAR THE SNOW CRUNCH,

(The beeping of a truck backing up. MAN tries to help guide the truck and almost gets hit by a truck.)

SEE THE KIDS BUNCH,
THIS IS SANTA'S BIG SCENE.

AND ABOVE ALL THIS BUSTLE YOU HEAR:

(A loud car screech!) What are you trying to do, kill me?!

SILVER BELLS,
(Jack hammer.)
SILVER BELLS
(Jack hammer.)
IT'S CHRISTMAS TIME ...

(The music pauses. MAN smiles as an ice cream truck goes by.)

IN THE CITY.
(Long jack hammer.)
RING A LING, HEAR THEM RING
SOON IT WILL BE CHRISTMAS DAY.

(No matter what MAN does he is bombarded by another sound.)

SILVER BELLS,
(A dog bark.)
SILVER BELLS
(He steps on a cat's tail. A cow moos.)
IT'S CHRISTMAS TIME IN THE CITY.
RING A LING
(He hears a gunshot and ducks.)
HEAR THEM RING
(An arrow flies near his head. The sounds build in absurdity to even include a 'Tarzan call.')
SOON IT WILL BE
SOON IT WILL BE
SOON IT WILL BE

(Finally it is silent. He is safe. He stands, pulls himself together ...)

CHRISTMAS DAY!

(WOMAN 3 enters in a Santa suit carrying a pail and ringing a bell. MAN 1 puts money in her bucket and asks for bell. She rings it once more. He takes it from her. He turns front.)

MAN 1. OY!

(Blackout. Lights come up on WOMAN 2 and MAN 2 in a loving embrace. They sing front. A light comes up on a small Christmas tree covered in lights that are not turned on.)

THIS WILL BE THE BEST CHRISTMAS EVER!

MAN 2.
THERE'S A CHILL IN THE AIR
   WOMAN 2.
A WARM GLOW FROM THE FIRE
   MAN 2.
THE SHOP WINDOWS BECKON
'COME BE THE NEXT BUYER'

   WOMAN 2.
A SEASON OF PEACE AND A HEAVENLY CHOIR
   MAN 2.
IT'S CHRISTMAS!
   WOMAN 2.
CHRISTMAS!

   BOTH.
CHRISTMAS
AND OUR ONE DESIRE ... IS THAT

(They walk to opposite sides of the stage to retrieve their boxes filled with Christmas ornaments. Her box is covered with wrapping paper and bows, his with duct tape and car oil stickers.)

THIS WILL BE THE BEST CHRISTMAS EVER!
TOGETHER AS A PAIR!

   MAN 2.
WE'LL HIT A HUNDRED STORES!
   WOMAN 2.
WE'LL CUDDLE EATING S'MORES!
   MAN 2.
THE SCENT OF AMEX PLATINUM SEEPING FROM MY PORES!

BOTH.
THIS WILL BE THE BEST CHRISTMAS EVER!

(She goes to her box.)

THIS WILL BE THE BEST CHRISTMAS EVER!
A TREE THAT'S ALL OUR OWN!

(She puts a bow on top of the tree, then circles the tree placing a popcorn garland around it.)

WOMAN 2.
A DELICATE DESIGN
   MAN 2.
A THOUSAND LIGHTS WILL SHINE!

(He plugs in tree. The tree is aglow with awful tacky colored lights.)

WOMAN 2.
LOVINGLY TRIMMED WITH POPCORN
   MAN 2.
A YULE-TIDE STAR WARS SHRINE!

(MAN 2 gets carried away and starts acting out his Star Wars fantasy ...with hanging plastic figurines from Episode II—Attack of the Clones! And for the top of the tree, light saber glowing like a halo— Grand Master Yoda! In his best Yoda voice:) "On top of the tree I must go." *(He places Yoda at the top of the tree.)* "Happy there I will be." *(He catches the look on WOMAN 2's face. Clearly she isn't happy.)* "Popcorn I must have." *(He takes the popcorn from her and places it on Yoda.)* "Holding a string of popcorn."

   BOTH.
IT WOULD BE DIVINE!
WHEN WE HAVE THE BEST CHRISTMAS EVER!

   WOMAN 2.
LETS FILL OUR HEARTS
WITH NEW-FOUND
SPIRITUALITY
   MAN 2.
LETS MAKE THAT DREAM OF

HIGH-DEF TV
A REALITY!

WOMAN 2.
MIDNIGHT MASS ON CHRISTMAS EVE
THE FEAST OF THE SEVEN FISH
    MAN 2.
WE'LL BLOW OFF MASS ON CHRISTMAS EVE
AND HOOK UP OUR SATELLITE DISH!

    WOMAN 2. You wish! *(She decides to hurry and fill the tree with her ornaments. He follows with his own ornaments. They race to fill the tree.)*
IF YOU WANT THE BEST CHRISTMAS EVER
    MAN 2.
TOGETHER WE WILL SHARE
    WOMAN 2.
WE'LL NESTLE HERE ALONE
AND DISCONNECT THE PHONE
    MAN 2.
WELL THROW THE WILDEST SHINDIG
THE WORLD HAS EVER KNOWN!

    BOTH.
THIS WILL BE THE BEST CHRISTMAS EVER!

(They look at each other as if in a face-off.)

THIS WILL BE THE BEST CHRISTMAS EVER!
IT'S MY GIFT TO YOU

    WOMAN 2.
WE'LL TOAST THE COMING YEAR!
    MAN 2.
WE'LL CHUG A CASE OF BEER!
    WOMAN 2.
A HOLY NIGHT OF PEACE
    MAN 2.
THE NEIGHBORS CALL POLICE
    WOMAN 2.
I'LL HOLD YOU TIGHT AND PRAY

MAN 2.
I'LL HOLD YOU TIGHT AND
   WOMAN 2.
HEY!

(They circle each other.)

   BOTH.
WELL SHARE SO MUCH THIS CHRISTMAS
LETS MAKE IT CHRISTMAS
EVERY DAY!

OK!

(It is clear that the tree is a mess. They each know what the problem is—the other persons ornaments! MAN goes first as they each run around the tree taking the other's ornaments off.)

THIS WILL BE THE BEST, BEST, CHRISTMAS
   MAN 2.
EVER
   WOMAN 2.
THIS WILL BE THE BEST CHRISTMAS EVER
   MAN 2.
THIS WILL BE THE BEST CHRISTMAS EVER
   WOMAN 2.
THIS WILL BE THE BEST CHRISTMAS EVER
   MAN 2.
THIS WILL BE THE BEST CHRISTMAS EVER
   WOMAN 2.
THIS WILL BE THE BEST CHRISTMAS EVER
   MAN 2.
THIS WILL BE THE BEST

(They stand there looking at the bare tree then at each other. WOMAN 2 picks up the one ornament left on the tree. It is hers. She wins. They each pick up a box and exit.
Party noise is heard from off stage. WOMAN 3 enters as if she is just leaving the party. She is wearing her coat and a piece of garland as a scarf. Clearly she has had a little too much to drink. She ad-libs as she exits.)

WOMAN 3. Great party. Thanks for inviting me! Don't forget to come to my party—next Tuesday night! Bye!

THE CHRISTMAS PARTY / I'D LIKE TO HITCH A RIDE WITH SANTA CLAUS

WOMAN 3.
IT'S A YULE TIDE BASH
THE EGGNOG IS GREAT
IT'S EIGHTY PROOF, JUST THE FOAM
SO, I'VE HAD TOO MUCH
AND IT'S GETTING LATE
BUT NO GUY WILL TAKE ME HOME
BUT THERE IS ONE GUY WHO COULD MAKE MY DAY
HE COULD GIVE ME A RIDE

(She climbs onto the piano.)

HE'S EVEN GOT A SLEIGH

(She crosses her legs and tells the audience her idea.)

I THINK I'LL HITCH A RIDE WITH SANTA CLAUS
WOULDN'T THAT BE SOMETHING TO SEE
I'D LIKE TO HITCH A RIDE WITH SANTA CLAUS
DODGING THE CLOUDS
WAVING AT CROWDS
I'D CRACK THE WHIP AND
KEEP A WATCH FOR WEATHER VANES

(She lays on the piano.)

I'D HELP HIM WITH HIS BAG
AND CHECK EACH CHRISTMAS TAG
OR MAYBE I COULD HANDLE THE REINS

(She turns on her back.)

I'D LIKE TO HITCH A RIDE WITH SANTA CLAUS
WOULDN'T THEY BE JEALOUS OF ME

THEY COULDN'T SAY I RAN AWAY
BECAUSE AFTER WE'D ROAM
HE'LL DRIVE ME HOME

(She sits back up and crosses her legs.)

AND WHEN THEY SEE ME CHRISTMAS MORNING
WHAT'LL I SAY WITH A LOOK OF DELIGHT?
I'M THE GIRL THAT RODE WITH SANTA CLAUS LAST NIGHT

(She slinks down off the piano and pulls her coat off her shoulders.)
All right, Mr. C, you ready to take me home? *(She struts back and throws her coat on the piano.)*

YOU BETTER WATCH OUT
YOU BETTER NOT CRY
YOU BETTER NOT POUT
I'M TELLIN' YOU WHY

(She crosses DSR.)

SANTA CLAUS IS COMING
COMING TO TOWN

(She crosses DSL.)

HE'S MAKING A LIST
CHECKING IT TWICE
GONNA FIND OUT WHO'S NAUGHTY OR NICE
SANTA CLAUS IS COMING
COMING TO TOWN

HE SEES YOU WHEN YOU'RE SLEEPING
HE KNOWS IF YOU'RE AWAKE
HE KNOWS IF YOU'VE BEEN BAD OR GOOD
SO BE GOOD FOR GOODNESS SAKE
    BAND.
FOR GOODNESS SAKE!

    WOMAN 3. *(Crossing up stage.)*
YOU BETTER WATCH OUT

YOU BETTER NOT CRY
YOU BETTER NOT POUT

(Turning front.)

I'M TELLIN' YOU WHY
SANTA CLAUS IS COMING

    BAND. Ho!

    WOMAN 3.
HE'S COMING

    BAND. Ho, Ho, Ho!

    WOMAN 3.
AND WHEN HE'S COMIN' HO! I'LL BE
HITCHIN' A RIDE WITH SANTA CLAUS
WOULDN'T THAT BE SOMETHING TO SEE
THEY COULDN'T SAY I RAN AWAY
BECAUSE AFTER WE ROAM

(She waves the boa over her head.)

HE'LL DRIVE ME HOME

    BAND.
AND WHEN THEY SEE HER CHRISTMAS MORNING
WHAT'LL SHE SAY WITH A LOOK OF DELIGHT?
    WOMAN 3.
YEAH, I'M THE GIRL THAT RODE WITH SANTA CLAUS
LAST NIGHT, SO YOU BETTER WATCH OUT

(She gets back up on the piano)

    BAND.
YEAH, SHE'S THE GIRL THAT RODE WITH SANTA CLAUS

    WOMAN 3. I just love a man with a beard. *(She ends the number in a sexy pose on the piano.)*
LAST NIGHT

(Applause. WOMAN 1 enters reading the book. WOMAN 3 sings to her, boasting.)

AND WHEN THEY SEE ME CHRISTMAS MORNING
WHAT'LL I SAY WITH A LOOK OF DELIGHT?
YA, I'M THE GIRL THAT RODE WITH SANTA CLAUS

(Noticing the time.) Oops! Gotta run. I have a date with the jolly man at the North Pole. I can't be late; he's got a whip.

(WOMAN 3 exits. WOMAN 1 is left on stage.)

WOMAN 1.
THERE GOES THE GIRL THAT RIDES
WITH SANTA CLAUS TONIGHT.

(She opens her book back up and reads as she walks to the piano and puts her book down.)

BOOK. The first step is always the hardest—your attitude. Affirm to yourself, right this minute that this is going to be your best holiday season ever. Go ahead. Say it out loud! "This is going to be my best holiday season ever!"
WOMAN 1. *(With little to no enthusiasm.)* This is going to be my best holiday ever.
BOOK. Congratulations! You're off to a great start. *(WOMAN 1 gives a sigh of relief.)* RELATIONSHIPS. *(WOMAN 1 gives a sigh of frustration.)* Reaching out to others is always a wonderful place to ….

(She closes her book. She looks at pianist. Slowly she walks her way over to him.)

WOMAN 1. *(Insert piano player's name here)*?
PIANO PLAYER. I'm married.
WOMAN 1. Of course. I wasn't ….
PIANO PLAYER. Not that I wouldn't. You're a lovely woman with a terrific ….
WOMAN 1. Save it!

(She slams the book down on the piano and the music begins.)

THE HAPPY NEW YEAR BLUES

WOMAN 1.
OUT IN THE STREET
HEAR THE BEAT OF A DRUM
IT'S TWELVE O'CLOCK AND THE NEW YEAR HAS COME
JUST HEAR THEM YELL
AS THEY WELCOME THE NEWS
I SHOULD BE GLAD BUT I'M NOT
'CUS I'M SAD 'CUS
I'VE GOT THE HAPPY NEW YEAR BLUES

(WOMAN 2 enters talking on her cell phone.)

WOMAN 2. Hi, this is *(Insert your name here)*. I'm responding to your personal ad. I was wondering, what are you looking for? *(To piano player.)* Could I pass for 19? *(PIANO PLAYER shakes his head "NO".)* I'm 20 … *(Piano Player continues to shake head 'NO'.)* 1 … 2 … 3 … *(Ignoring PIANO PLAYER.)* 21 through 23, somewhere in my early 20s … to mid 20s—below 30. I'm in very good shape for my age, work out every day. Of course I'm a blonde! Of course I'd love to be spanked, what! *(Realizing what she just said, She yells.)* You creep! *(She hangs up and crosses behind piano.)*

THE VERY FIRST OF EACH JANUARY
KEEPS GETTING WORSE
'CUS I HAVE TO CARRY
ONE MORE YEAR
WITH NOBODY NEAR
WHO FEELS JUST THE SAME AS I

(MAN 1 enters.)

MAN 1. *(Reading back cover of book.)* Other Books by author: "Searching for Your Soul Mate," "Finding that Special Romance," "Embracing Your Dog."
PIANO PLAYER. Embracing your …?
MAN 1. Don't knock it till you've tried it, married man.

OUT IN THE STREET THE CROWD WALKING
SHOUTING A HIP HURRAY

FILLING THE NIGHT WITH LOVE, TALKING
I SEEM TO HEAR THEM SAY

(He crosses downstage.)

HERE COMES OLD FATHER TIME
BRINGING PLENTY OF HAPPY NEWS
EVERYONE'S GLAD WHILE I'M SINGING
THE HAPPY NEW YEAR BLUES

(WOMAN 3 enters reading book then shuts it.)

WOMAN 3. It's impossible to meet anyone during the holidays. Everyone's so happy and gay or happy *and* gay!
PIANO PLAYER. Not that there's anything wrong with that.
WOMAN 3. Easy for you to say, married man.

A WEDDING RING
A SWEET BRIDAL BOUQUET
AND EVERYTHING I KNOW WOULD BE OK
BUT EACH DAY IT'S FURTHER AWAY
AND MY HOW THE TIME DOES FLY

(She backs up and sits on the bench with the PIANO PLAYER. MAN 2 enters from the back of the house. He addresses the audience.)

MAN 2. Okay. This one is for the ladies in the audience. I need to see a show of hands. How many of you are interested in a quiet dinner for two at a five-star restaurant? Wonderful. How many .... *(Pointing to a man in the audience.)* Put your hand down, sir. How many *women* would be interested in island hopping through the Caribbean on our own personal yacht? Sir, no. Excellent! How many of you lovely ladies are interested in financially supporting—yours truly? *(The music stops.)* No one? *(The music starts up again.)*

COUNTING THE DAYS UNTIL
SOMEONE GIVES ME SOME SYMPATHY
Buddy, you still interested?
HOPING TO GET A THRILL
FROM ONE WHO'LL GET A THRILL FROM ME
Leave your number at the box office.

ALL.
YEAR AFTER YEAR I GROW OLDER
SOON THEY WILL ALL BE GONE
GOING THROUGH LIFE WITH NO SHOULDER
TO LAY MY HEAD UPON

(They all bow their heads.)

PIANO PLAYER. Perhaps a slight adjustment in your attitudes would ....

(Their heads pop up as they yell at the PIANO PLAYER.)

ALL. Shut up, married man. *(They all move DS into a "V" formation.)*

BRING OUT THE OLD YEAR AND RING IN THE NEW
MEANS NOTHING TO SOMEONE WHO FEELS SO BLUE
THERE GOES MY PHONE
BUT IT'S NOT HAPPY NEWS
CENTRAL IS RINGING MY PHONE JUST TO WISH ME
A HAPPY NEW YEAR BLUES
A VERY HAPPY NEW YEAR BLUES

(One by one they exit the stage leaving the PIANO PLAYER on stage alone in a spotlight. Interested in finding out what all the fuss is about, he picks up the book and reads.)

BOOK. Holiday Dieting: A high protein, low carb diet can .... *(He turns the page.)* The Season of Giving: Ten percent of your gross income could .... *(He turns the page again.)* Taking Control of Your Holiday Destiny: Do you feel overworked and under appreciated? Do you follow while others lead? Are others stepping into your spotlight? If you've answered yes to any or all of these questions, then it's time to stop thinking of yourself as a lowly elf! Take charge of your Holiday Destiny and start thinking of yourself as Santa Claus himself ... *(He looks up from the book and rubs his chin a la David Letterman. Dream music is heard as he thinks ...)* as Santa Claus himself ... as Santa Claus himself ....

(With a new determination, he places the Santa hat on his head and

breaks into song.)

REINDEER BOOGIE / JINGLE BELLS

SANTA (PIANO PLAYER).
SANTA HAD A CUP OF COFFEE
AND HE ATE A LITTLE SNACK
THREW HIS OLD PACK RIGHT OVER HIS BACK
OPEN THE WINDOWS OF HIS LITTLE SHACK
AND SHOUTED OH DASHER AND DANCER

Dasher! Dancer! Comet! Cupid!

(WOMEN 1 and MAN 1 enter wearing antlers and warm up, very unenthusiastically.)

HEY BLITZEN COME ON OVER HERE

(MAN 2 enters wearing reindeer antler, finishing his cigarette and carrying a cup of coffee.)

WE'RE GONNA GET A-GOIN'
AND SPREAD SOME CHEER
SO LIMBER UP YOUR LEGS
AND SHARPEN YOUR HOOVES
CAUSE TONIGHT IS THE NIGHT
WE'RE GONNA JUMP ON THE ROOVES

WELL THE REINDEER
THEY WERE SO PROUD AND GRAND
TO TAKE ANOTHER TRIP ALL OVER THE LAND
THEY JUMPED RIGHT INTO THEIR PROPER PLACE
TO GET HEPPED UP FOR THAT MIDNIGHT RACE

(ACTORS ad-lib as they get in line. MAN 2 is the last to get in line.)

THEY STARTED SINGING ...

(The REINDEER, too pooped to partake, just stand there. The PIANO PLAYER tries again ...) They started singing!

(Reluctantly, quietly, they sing.)

REINDEER.
JINGLE BELLS, JINGLE BELLS

SANTA. Thank you.

REINDEER.
JINGLE ALL THE WAY

SANTA. And dancing ....

REINDEER.
OH WHAT FUN IT IS TO RIDE
IN ONE HORSE OPEN SLEIGH

SANTA. A little faster ....

REINDEER & SANTA.
JINGLE BELLS, JINGLE BELLS
JINGLE ALL THE WAY
OH WHAT FUN IT IS TO RIDE
IN A ONE HORSE OPEN SLEIGH

PIANO PLAYER. *(Handing a red nose off to one of the ACTORS, the PIANO PLAYER asks:)* Okay, who's Rudolph, this year?

(Not wanting to be the one left holding the nose, the ACTORS pass it along from one to the other until the last one gets an idea, runs up to an unsuspecting AUDIENCE MEMBER:)

ACTOR. Excuse me, won't you guide our sleigh tonight?

(The ACTOR puts the nose and a set of antlers on the AUDIENCE MEMBER and makes her or him them dance along with them.)

SANTA.
OL' SANTA HE SHOOK OFF THAT ICE AND SNOW
BOARDED HIS SLEIGH
AND THEN YELLED, "LET'S GO!"

ALL THE LITTLE TOYS WERE HAPPY TOO
'CAUSE THEY WERE SO BRIGHT AND NEW
   REINDEER.
BRIGHT AND NEW

   SANTA.
A LITTLE PIANO THEN STARTED TO PLAY
OH SANTA BEGAN TO SWING AND SWAY
THOUGHT HE HEARD
A TOY DRUM STARTIN' TO BEAT

   WOMAN 3. Tap solo, Rudolph!

(They all stop and point at RUDOLPH's feet.)

   SANTA.
BUT HE FOUND IT WAS THE RHYTHM
OF THE REINDEER FEET

   REINDEER. Conga! *(The ACTORS grab AUDIENCE MEMBER and make him or her lead the conga line.)*

JINGLE BELLS, JINGLE BELLS
JINGLE ALL THE WAY
OH WHAT FUN IT IS TO RIDE
IN A ONE HORSE OPEN SLEIGH

   REINDEER & SANTA.
JINGLE BELLS, JINGLE BELLS
JINGLE ALL THE WAY
OH WHAT FUN IT IS TO RIDE
IN A ONE HORSE OPEN SLEIGH
OH WHAT FUN IT IS TO RIDE
IN A ONE HORSE OPEN SLEIGH
OH WHAT FUN IT IS TO RIDE
IN A ONE HORSE OPEN SLEIGH

Big Finish!!

   SANTA.
DO THE REINDEER BOOGIE

THIS CHRISTMAS EVE NIGHT

(All end around RUDOLPH. WOMAN 2 exits. MAN 1 grabs the Polaroid camera from off stage and takes a picture of our volunteer and the other reindeer. He gives the audience member the photo as WOMEN 1 and 3 escort him or her back to his or her seat as the lights fade to black. In the dark we hear:)

BOOK. By the time the clock strikes twelve on Christmas Eve, construction will have been completed on approximately 17 million Barbie Dream Houses, 473 miles of track will be laid for the over 9 million train sets sold, and enough batteries will have been purchased to power the state of Rhode Island ... for the remainder of the year. Your tree is trimmed, *(Lights up on WOMAN 2 center stage.)* stockings hung, kids tucked into bed, and sugar plumbs or not, this is the perfect opportunity to take a moment for yourself. *(MUSIC CUE.)* For rest assured, tomorrow morning you will be awakened by the magic of Christmas.

CHRISTMAS EVE

WOMAN 2.
CHRISTMAS, CHRISTMAS, CHRISTMAS EVE.
IN MY HEART I STILL BELIEVE
THAT THE WORLD IS A LOVING PLACE.

AS I DECORATE THE TREE,
I RECALL THE CHILD IN ME
WHEN THE WORLD WAS A LOVING PLACE

OH THE PRESENTS
FROM MY MOTHER.
OH THE PRESENTS
FROM MY DAD.

ALL THAT WRAPPING
AND UNWRAPPING
THE BEST GIFT I EVER HAD.
LET ME PASS IT ON TO YOU MY CHILD
AS YOU DREAM OF GIFTS TO COME.

TAKE THIS LOVE ALONG YOUR JOURNEY AND
DON'T FORGET
WHERE YOU CAME FROM.

PRAY FOR THE ONES
WHO ARE LESS FORTUNATE THAN WE ARE.
PRAY FOR THE ONES WHO ARE IN NEED.
LIVE EVERY DAY AS IF IT MIGHT BE YOUR LAST DAY.
LET LOVING-KINDNESS BE YOUR CREED.

SOMEDAY WE WILL ALL BE FREE.
CHRISTMAS FOR ETERNITY,
IN A WORLD THAT'S A LOVING PLACE.

I FEEL THE PRESENCE
OF MY MOTHER.
AND THE PRESENCE
OF MY DAD.
ALL THAT WRAPPING
AND UNWRAPPING
THE BEST GIFT I EVER HAD.

LET ME PASS IT ON TO YOU MY CHILD
AS YOU DREAM OF GIFTS TO COME.
TAKE THIS LOVE ALONG YOUR JOURNEY AND
NEVER FORGET
WHERE YOU CAME FROM.

(Fade to black.
A lighting special appears on the floor in the shape of a square, representing an elevator. Whenever someone pushes the elevator button, the PIANO PLAYER plays a note on the piano. WOMAN 3 enters and crosses to elevator door carrying packages; she pushes the button. MAN 2 enters carrying a large shopping bag. In a rush, he hits the button three times. Ignoring each other and turning front, they read the book.)

BOOK. According to a recent poll of holiday shoppers, the second greatest fear during "The Season of Giving" is balancing one's checkbook! *(WOMAN 1 and MAN 1 now enter in the midst of an argument about their purchases—they become quieter as they near*

the elevator, finally shutting up. Sound Effect: Ding. Elevator doors open. The four step into the elevator. They each push a button. As the doors are about to shut, WOMAN 2 rushes on and to the elevator. Using her purse to stop the door, it reopens. She steps in with the others. She pushes a button but it's the wrong one so she pushes another, irritating the others. The doors shut. Elevator musak begins. They all pull out their books and read. IT'S BEGINNING TO LOOK A LOT LIKE CHRISTMAS, *musical underscoring—prerecorded.)*
... The first greatest fear of the holiday season, surprisingly enough, is *not* getting invited to Christmas parties.

(Sound effect: elevator DING!)

FEMALE VOICEOVER. Third floor—Auto Parts, Garden Equipment, Ladies' Lingerie.

(Doors open, WOMAN 1 and MAN 1 exit elevator. Doors close. THEY pick up with their argument. Musak.)

BOOK. Combine these two issues, and it's enough to bring even George Baily to the bridge.

(Sound effect: elevator DING! As MAN 2 chuckles, WOMAN 2 catches him. They smile at each other for a moment.)

FEMALE VOICEOVER. Seventh floor—Home Electronics, Office Furniture, Ladies' Lingerie.

(Doors open, WOMAN 3 nearly plows over WOMAN 2 as they both exit the elevator. The doors close. Musak.)

BOOK. Well here's a way to kill two turtledoves with one stone. Not only is it a great way to sock away some extra cash, it's also guaranteed to be an exciting and fun way to meet new and interesting people: Seasonal Employment.

(Sound effect: elevator DING!)

FEMALE VOICEOVER. Tenth floor—Customer Service, Santa's Village!
MAN 2. Ladies' Lingerie.

FEMALE VOICEOVER. ... and of course, Ladies' Lingerie.

(Sound effect: doors open. MAN 2 exits elevator.)

BOOK. Seasonal Employment can take many forms ....

(Sound effect: elevator doors close. Music begins.)

SANTA FANTASY

(MAN 2 pushes his 'Santa Throne' into place. He is sort of small and thin to cut a Santa figure himself but nevertheless full of enthusiasm.)

MAN 2. Ah yes, very important job to do today. Yes siree, can't have the Christmas Season without me! There's only one man who is totally indispensable during the big Christmas rush.

EV'RY YEAR GROWING UP
SOME GROWNUP IN OUR FAMILY
GOT TO BE—SANTA
GOT TO PUT ON THE RED SUIT

(He pulls a Santa suit out of his bag.)

WHITE BEARD AND HAT
MAKE AN ENTRANCE,
HO, HO, HO AND ALL THAT

PLAY THE ROLE
ON CHRISTMAS EVE
LETTING ALL US KIDS BELIEVE
IN SANTA—A FANTASY
HOW I LONGED TO SOMEDAY BE
SANTA

(Putting on a white beard and checking himself in a mirror, he likes what he sees. He begins to prepare for the role of a lifetime and tries out his acting skills.) Ah yes, tis a far, far better thing that I do now than I have ever done before. Ho, Ho, Ho!

PIANIST. Okay, Olivier, your public awaits. Time is money.

MAN 2. Coming! *(He continues to dress as Santa.)*

WELL I'VE YET TO BE CAST
AS THE MASTER HIMSELF
THOUGH THREE YEARS I'VE PASSED,
PILING TOYS ON A SHELF
AND BEING HARASSED WHILE PLAYING AN ELF
NOW THIS TIME—LOOK I'M ...

(He is now fully dressed.)

SANTA!
KIDS, I'LL MAKE ALL YOUR DREAMS COME TRUE
GONNA CHARM THE PANTS OFF YOUR PARENTS TOO
I'M SANTA
A FANTASY COMIN' TRUE
OOOOOO

NOW I'M ... SANTA!
GONNA MAKE HISTORY TODAY
SALES WILL SOAR CAUSE I'M HERE TO STAY
I'M SANTA—YOUR FANTASY COME TRUE ....

PIANIST. Shakespeare, there's a kid already waiting .
MAN 2. Yes, yes, it's Showtime, folks!!! *(MAN 2 sits down to greet the first customer: a puppet that he pulls from his bag. He is very excited to finally be playing the role. He operates the puppet himself while the voice is supplied on tape.)* Well, ho, ho, ho! Someone must have gotten up pretty early to see Old Santa.
LITTLE BOY. Not really. My mother works in Ladies Lingerie.
MAN 2. Oh?
LITTLE BOY. Maidenform, two for one.
MAN 2. *(Vamping. A little nervous. He didn't expect this answer.)* OK ... alrighty then, little boy why don't you tell Ooold Santa here what you want for Christmas.
LITTLE BOY. Well ... for starters, a new color Gameboy, a Sony digital camera and maybe a new powerbook, anything Harry Potter and ....

MAN 2.
I'LL LISTEN AND GRIN AND I'LL TAKE IN HIS LIST

WHILE I GLISTEN WITHIN, FULL OF JOY THAT I'VE MISSED
YES, THIS IS THE REASON WHY I EXIST!
THIS TIME, LOOK I'M ....
    SANTA.
KID, I'LL MAKE ALL YOUR DREAMS COME TRUE
CENTER STAGE WITH A JOB TO DO
I'M SANTA
MY FANTASIES COMIN' TRUE
OOOOOO—

(LITTLE BOY pulls on his beard.) OW!! Hey, what are you doing?

LITTLE BOY. *(Tugging again on MAN 2's beard.)* Is this thing glued on??
MAN 2. What??
LITTLE BOY. You need some spirit gum.
MAN 2. Huh?
LITTLE BOY. My mom used it on my Dumbledore costume for Halloween. It works great. You just need a little dab on the edges ....

MAN 2. *(Readjusting his beard.)*
I'M SANTA
KID, YOU'RE BLOWING MY COVER HERE
LET ME DO THIS FOR ONCE THIS YEAR
LET SANTA
HAVE A FANTASY COME TRUE

LITTLE BOY. You better get one of those elves to run up to Linens and Bedding and get you a pillow to stuff in that suit. Looks like Santa spent the summer with Jenny Craig.
MAN 2. Now come on there, little boy.
LITTLE BOY. O.K. cut the little boy stuff. You and I both know there is no Santa Claus and you are just last years elf in a big red suit making what? Ten dollars an hour?
MAN 2. Twenty.
LITTLE BOY. Not bad. But listen buddy, nobody's gonna bring me all those things I was listing and nobody's gonna bring my dad home this Christmas either. See ya.

(He turns to leave.)

MAN 2. I guess if you really don't believe in old Santa here,

there's nothing I can do to change your mind. But ya gotta have dreams, kid.
    LITTLE BOY. I do?
    MAN 2. Sure. I did.
    LITTLE BOY. Yeah ....
    MAN 2. And look where it got me!
    LITTLE BOY. *(Cutting him to the quick.)* Right.

MAN 2.
NO USE WONDERING WHAT'S REAL OR NOT
MAYBE THIS SANTA'S NOT ALL THAT HOT
BUT DREAMS GET YOU THROUGH
AND SOME DAYS THEY DO COME TRUE

    LITTLE BOY. Yeah, well ... maybe I'll see ya again tomorrow. Don't forget to try the spirit gum.
    MAN 2. Thanks for the tip, kid. See ya soon. *(MAN 2 stuffs the puppet back in the shopping bag.)*

I'M SANTA
JUST A GUY WITH A JOB TO DO
JUST A LIE FOR A WEEK OR TWO
I'M SANTA
A FANTASY ...

SO WHAT, I'M ... SANTA
CHANGE YOUR LIFE? MAYBE NOT THIS YEAR
BUT SITTING HERE I CAN SPREAD SOME CHEER
I'M SANTA- MY FANTASY COMIN'
SANTA, YOUR FANTASY COMIN'
SANTA, A FANTASY COME TRUE!

    PIANIST. Leibowitz, keep it moving!
    MAN 2. Next?

SILENT NIGHT (Music Underscore) / SKETCH OF SANTA'S VILLAGE

(WOMAN 2 sheepishly enters. She is wearing a leopard scarf with matching handbag, gloves and dark sunglasses.)

SANTA (MAN 2). Ho, Ho, Ho! Welcome to The North Pole. *(Looking for a child.)* No need to hide behind mommy. Is someone being shy today?

WOMAN 2. Yes. Yes, I am.

SANTA. ... Beg your pardon.

WOMAN 2. I don't have any children, but ... I won't go into that just yet, see I thought ....

SANTA. Security!

WOMAN 2. Sit down! I paid that pushy little elf 20 bucks for two minutes with you and I'm not leaving until .... *(He stands.)* I said sit down!

SANTA. Look, lady ....

WOMAN 2. *(Sits on his lap, pulls a piece of paper from her purse.)* Humor me.

SANTA. Ho, ho, ho. You wrote out a list? Ho, ho, ho.

WOMAN 2. Thought I'd save you some time. These are the things I need. *(Trying to calm herself, she takes in her surroundings.)* Wow, as a kid I always imagined "Santa's World" much bigger. Everything's so tiny!

SANTA. *(Reading from the paper.)* You need your septic tank pumped and flushed. A generous contribution to your 401K.

WOMAN 2. Both of them.

SANTA. ... Repair or replace your catalytic converter to meet with New York State Emission Standards.

WOMAN 2. I also need a palm pilot that receives email but I didn't want to appear pushy. *(She gets up off SANTA's lap.)* There. I've done it. Thank you for your consideration. Good bye.

(She starts to exit. He stands.)

SANTA. What about the things you want?

WOMAN 2. I beg your pardon?

SANTA. Want. That's why you come to Santa— to tell him the things you want, not the things you need.

WOMAN 2. *(Thinking it over.)* Oh. Oh, I see. Want. Well, I don't know what I want. I haven't given it much .... Maybe a .... There must be .... God, how do kids put up with this pressure?

SANTA. Some advice, why don't you ....

WOMAN 2. *(Crossing stage right.)* No! I got enough advice. I talked to that Salvation Army Santa for three hours yesterday. Three hours! You know what advice that looser gave me, "Visit your friends!" Well, I don't have any friends! I try. I do. But, apparently I scare people.

SANTA. Really?

WOMAN 2. So put that down, "I—want—friends."

SANTA. Lady, I'm not a therapist.

WOMAN 2. Oh, no. You're just Santa Claus. Mr. Jolly and nice. Judging all the rest of us losers from the tenth floor of a department store for ten bucks an hour. You're not some pathetic washout who can't even find a date for the office Christmas party. Can I smoke in here?

SANTA. The elf smoking lounge is ....

WOMAN 2. I just don't know how to meet people.

SANTA. That's tough for everyone.

WOMAN 2. Not *you*. All you *do* is meet people .... *(He indicates with his hand how tall the children are.)* Oh, yeah. I don't know how you do it. I'm not very good with children.

SANTA. Really? Me either. Twenty bucks an hour.

WOMAN 2. Santa's doing okay.

SANTA. Seasonal.

WOMAN 2. Well ... *(Looking at her watch.)* I've got a three o'clock. Thanks for listening. It's just that, this book said if you just ask .... Every year at work, our Christmas Party. Ten years. No date.

SANTA. I'm sorry.

WOMAN 2. How about you? Got a date for your Christmas gathering.

SANTA. *(He laughs. His laugh turns into "HO! HO! HO!" when he realizes he might be heard. Quieter:)* Santa's Jewish.

WOMAN 2. Good for you—less pressure. I can't find anyone to put up with me. Men say I'm too strong. Too threatening.

SANTA. Women usually complain I'm not aggressive enough.

(They both laugh.)

WOMAN 2. What are you doing next Thursday?
SANTA. I'm off at five.
WOMAN 2. How would you like to ....
SANTA. Yes.

(MUSIC CUE. They are looking in each other's eyes. She looks at her watch, realizing she has to go. She pulls out a card.)

WOMAN 2. You won't be disappointed. It really is a fun party.

Here's my card. I can introduce you as ....
SANTA. A wish facilitator.
WOMAN 2. Oh ... that's good. *(Starts to leave, then turns back.)* You never know, do you.
SANTA. No, you don't.

(WOMAN 2 walks down stage center as if to leave, she stops in a pool of light, looks up and mouths, "thank you." As she exits, lights fade to black.
Lights up on PIANO PLAYER reading book.)

BOOK. Home for the Holidays! Remember, it's only once a year. So .... *(PIANO PLAYER turns page shaking his head "No.")* Buying your loved one that perfect gift. Money should be no object when .... *(PIANO PLAYER turns page shaking his head "No.")* Feeling abandoned at this, the most stressful of the holidays? Don't be afraid to ask for help from those around you. Think of yourself as Santa Claus himself with his built in support structure; subservient reindeer, helpful elves, and even Mrs. Santa Claus herself, Mrs. Santa Claus herself, Mrs. Santa Claus herself ....

(WOMAN 3 enters wearing a bathrobe, fluffy slippers, and her hair in curlers. She drags along a chair behind her.)

SURABAYA SANTA

WOMAN 3. *(A la Marlena Dietrich.)*
I WAS JUST SEVENTEEN
WHEN YOU RODE INTO TOWN
JUST A GIRL FULL OF FANTASIES AND LONGINGS
I SAW YOU
I KNEW I HAD TO BE WITH YOU

THEN YOU LOOKED IN MY EYES
AND YOU ASKED ME MY NAME
AND I TREMBLED BEFORE YOU LIKE A BABY

AND GENTLY I KISSED YOU
WHO COULD RESIST YOU
YOU TOOK ME HEART AND SOUL

and gave me the clap-per.

(She claps twice. Lights change dramatically to spot on her.)

AND BEFORE I HAD A CHANCE TO TAKE CONTROL
WE RETIRED TO YOUR PALACE ON THE POLE
WHERE WE ONLY HAD OURSELVES
AND THE REINDEER AND THE ELVES
AND A LOT OF THINGS WE NEVER SAID
ABOUT THE LIFE I COULD HAVE LEAD
IF I HAD HAD THE SENSE TO STAY AWAY
BUT HERE WE ARE NICK
AND SO, NICK
I KNOW IT'S TIME FOR YOU TO GO NICK
I KNOW BY NOW I'LL NEVER CLAIM YOU FOR MY OWN
I'VE BEEN RESIGNED TO SPEND MY CHRISTMASES ALONE

AND SO *AU REVOIR* NICK
IT'S GRAND NICK
I DON'T PRETEND TO UNDERSTAND NICK
I SAW YOU LOOK AT BLITZEN LONG AND LOVINGLY
THE WAY YOU USED TO LOOK AT ME

Oh, Nick, Nick, why don't you love me anymore? I've tried everything to keep myself attractive. I've got eight-minute abs, buns of steel and squeezed my way through thigh master, thigh mister and thigh misses. Six months eating nothing but reindeer patties and a side of cheese and look at me … I'm your little sugarplum again. *(She claps twice and is hit with more light.)* Thin as a peppermint stick, Nick. *(She steps off chair and crosses DS.)* Please take me with you. I'm just going crazy all cooped up in here. I won't take up much room. You won't even know I'm there. Damn it! Isn't there one ounce of human decency buried beneath all those layers of fat?! You disgust me! Oh, yes, it's so easy to judge, isn't it—deciding who's naughty and who's nice. Well who died and left you God, Mr. Claus! *(She grabs a suitcase and starts to pack up her robe, curlers and decorations.)*

BUT NEVER MIND, NICK
OKAY, NICK
I'D HATE TO KEEP YOU FROM YOUR SLEIGH, NICK
WHEN YOU RETURN I WILL BE MANY MILES AWAY

I'LL HAVE MY LAWYER CALL YOUR LAWYER
NEW YEAR'S DAY

THAT'S ALL FOR ME, NICK
GANG WAY, NICK
I'LL MISS YOU LESS THAN I CAN SAY, NICK
HAVE FUN WITH ALL THE LITTLE BOYS ALONG YOUR ROUTE
I'LL GET THE MANSION AND THE FACTORY TO BOOT
I WILL NOT WAIT UNTIL THE SNOW BENEATH ME THAWS
I WILL ESCAPE
YOUR SANTA

(She starts to exit but is stopped by the string of lights still connected offstage.)

CLAWS!

(On button she yanks the string of lights—blackout.
WOMAN 3 exits. MAN 1 enters from the back of the house wearing a ridiculous Christmas/Elvis outfit.)

SANTA CLAUS IS BACK IN TOWN

MAN 1. *(A la Elvis.)* Wow! My wife is one Christmas bummer, man! You know what this room needs is a E7 chord.

CHRISTMAS

I mean she gets so tense around the holidays. Must be her time of the year. *(Rim shot.)* Santa's feeling kind of lonely.

(WOMEN 1 and 2 run out to back up SANTA dressed like sexy candy canes.)

SANTA & WOMEN 1 & 2.
CHRISTMAS

MAN 1. I mean I don't know why she gets so upset. It's only one night. Santa needs a little sumthin' for Christmas too, you know. *(WOMAN 3 runs on obviously late. MAN 1 notices WOMAN 3. He does *a double take.)* Hey, you look exactly like my …. Oh, never mind.

ALL.
CHRISTMAS, OOO …

   MAN 1. A one, two, three, four …
WELL IT'S CHRISTMAS TIME PRETTY BABY
THE SNOW IS FALLIN' ON THE GROUND
   WOMEN.
CHRISTMAS TIME, CHRISTMAS TIME
   MAN 1.
WELL IT'S CHRISTMAS TIME PRETTY BABY
THE SNOW IS FALLIN' ON THE GROUND
   WOMEN.
CHRISTMAS TIME, CHRISTMAS TIME
   MAN 1.
YOU BEEN A REAL GOOD LITTLE BABY
SANTA CLAUS IS BACK IN TOWN

GOT NO SLEIGH WITH REINDEER
GOT NO SACK ON MY BACK
YOU GONNA SEE ME COMIN'
IN A BIG BLACK CADILLAC
   WOMEN.
YEAH … AH …

   MAN 1. *(To an unsuspecting AUDIENCE MEMBER.)* Do you believe in Santa Claus? Do you like fat men with whips? Honey one night with me, and you'll be seeing flying reindeer!

	WOMEN.
YEAH, IT'S CHRISTMAS PRETTY BABY	YEAH
THE SNOW IS FALLIN' ON THE GROUND	OOO…

   WOMEN.
CHRISTMAS TIME, CHRISTMAS TIME
   MAN 1.
YEAH, IT'S CHRISTMAS PRETTY BABY
LOOK AT THAT SNOW THERE ON THE GROUND
   WOMEN.
CHRISTMAS TIME, CHRISTMAS TIME
   MAN 1.
YOU BEEN A REAL GOOD LITTLE BABY

SANTA CLAUS IS BACK IN TOWN

HANG UP YOUR PRETTY STOCKIN'S
PUT OUT THE LIGHT
SANTA CLAUS IS COMIN' DOWN YOUR CHIMNEY TONIGHT
    WOMEN.
UH-HUH ...

    MAN 1. *(To another unsuspecting AUDIENCE MEMBER.)* Oh, yeah. Now, I've seen you when you're sleeping and I got two words for you—"pa-jamas!"

    WOMEN.
UH-HUH ...

IT'S CHRISTMAS PRETTY BABY
AND THE SNOW IS ON THE GROUND
    ALL.
YEAH, IT'S CHRISTMAS TIME
AND THE SNOW IS FALLIN'
DOWN, DOWN, DOWN, DOWN, DOWN, DOWN, DOWN
    MAN 1.
YOU BEEN A REAL GOOD LITTLE BABY
    WOMAN 1.
YOU BETTER WATCH OUT
    WOMAN 2.
YOU BETTER NOT CRY
    WOMAN 3.
YOU BETTER NOT POUT
    MAN 1.
I'LL TELL YOU WHY
'CAUSE I'VE MADE A LIST, CHECKED IT TWICE
LET'S BE NAUGHTY
    WOMEN.
BE NICE
    ALL.
SANTA CLAUS IS BACK IN TOWN
    MAN 1.
YEAH, YOU'VE BEEN A REAL GOOD LITTLE BABY
SANTA CLAUS, SANTA CLAUS IS

(MAN 2 crosses stage in a authentic Santa outfit.)

MAN 1. Hey! Who the heck are you!
MAN 2. The Easter Bunny.
MAN 1. Yeah, right. Everybody knows there is no Easter Bunny.

(MAN 2 exits.)

SANTA CLAUS IS BACK ... IN TOWN!

Sing it, girls!

WOMEN.	**MAN 1.**
CHRISTMAS TIME	
	These are my elves.
HO, HO, HO.	
	Nice legs.
SANTA CLAUS	
	Pointy ears.
MISTLETOE	
	(Kiss.)
JINGLE BELLS	
	Shake it ...
DECK THE HALLS	
	Fa, la, la , la
LITTLE ELVES	
	Sit on my lap!
SHINY BALLS	

MAN 1. Yes, that is a candy cane in my pocket, and I'm always happy to see you!

ALL.
YEAH!!!

MAN 1. Ladies and Gentlemen, Santa Claus has left the building!

(MAN 1 leaves, comes back, gives music cutoff cue. Blackout.)

END OF ACT ONE

ACT II

Entré Act

(As the Entré Act buttons, the Christmas lights flicker and go out with a typical electrical sound. A STAGEHAND with cup of coffee enters with headset and pretends to speak to the booth. He locates the bulb which is the culprit, gives it a turn, and all the lights come back on. The BAND concludes the Entré Act as the stagehand takes a bow and exits.
The stage goes dark as the band plays the last few bars of "Ave Maria." As the music concludes, a spotlight reveals a single microphone on a stand, center stage. MAN 2 enters into light and addresses audience.)

MAN 2. Let's hear it for Barbra Streisand's beautiful rendition of "Ave Maria." One of the best lip-sinking jobs I've ever seen. Thanks Fred. All right, who's next? There we go. Come on up. Don't be shy. *(WOMAN 2 enters from the audience. She looks uncomfortable. Whispered to WOMAN 2:)* Merde.

(MAN 2 exits.)

WOMAN 2. Hello, my name is *(Insert your name here, WOMAN 2)*.
MUSICIANS & OFFSTAGE ACTORS. Hi, *(Insert Woman 2's name here)*.
WOMAN 2. There are a few people here I'd like to thank for allowing me to perform in the pageant tonight.... Let me say that everyone here at the clinic has been so supportive. One person has been especially ... well, I think this explains how I feel. *(She nods at the piano player and sings. She's obviously uncomfortable in front of an audience of her peers.)*

THE TWELVE STEPS OF CHRISTMAS

FOR THE FIRST STEP OF CHRISTMAS
MY SPONSOR GAVE TO ME
A SESSION WITH HIS THERAPIST, TED.

FOR THE SECOND STEP OF CHRISTMAS
MY SPONSOR GAVE TO ME
TWO SHOPPING SPREES
I have the best sponsor.
AND A SESSION WITH HIS THERAPIST, TED

FOR THE THIRD STEP OF CHRISTMAS
MY SPONSOR GAVE TO ME
The serenity to accept the things I cannot change—The courage to change the things I can—And the wisdom to know the difference.
TWO SHOPPING SPREES
AND A SESSION WITH *MY* THERAPIST, TED

FOR THE FOURTH STEP OF CHRISTMAS
MY SPONSOR GAVE TO ME
FOUR KARATE CLASSES!
(She demonstrates with a loud scream "Hi-yah!")
Serenity to accept things I cannot change. Courage to change things I can. And wisdom to know the difference.
TWO SHOPPING SPREES
AND A SESSION WITH—TEDDY

FOR THE FIFTH STEP OF CHRISTMAS
MY SPONSOR GAVE TO ME
FIVE SMOKING PATCHES
They really work!
FOUR KARATE CLASSES
(A smaller demonstration, smaller scream. "Yah!")
The serenity, the courage, the wisdom...
TWO SHOPPING SPREES
AND A SESSION WITH ...

(She pulls the mic out of the stand. She is becoming more "showbizzy" and starts to work the crowd.) You know, Teddy and I have a relationship built on trust. He's such a good listener. It's so nice to have someone to share my life with ... *(She indicates to band to pick it up.)*

FOR THE SIXTH STEP OF CHRISTMAS
MY SPONSOR GAVE TO ME
SIX DATES WITH HIS BROTHER

(With one authoritative gesture, she cuts off the band.) His name is Russell, he's a doctor, and he has a full head of hair!

FIVE SMOKING PATCHES
Still working!
FOUR KARATE CLASSES
The serenity, so on and so forth ...
TWO SHOPPING SPREES
AND A SESSION WITH MY THERAPIST ...
Sometimes, Dr. T is a little late. Oh well, I don't really mind. I pay for the whole session. He's worth it. Trust. Our relationship is based on...

THE SEVENTH STEP OF CHRISTMAS
MY SPONSOR GAVE TO ME
SEVEN SHIATSU SESSIONS
SIX DATES WITH HIS BROTHER
FIVE SMOKING PATCHES
FOUR KARATE CLASSES
The Serenity, blah, blah, blah ...
TWO SHOPPING SPREES
AND A SESSION WITH ...

(She grabs the mic stand, dragging it behind her as she opens up to her public.) Trust! It's a street that runs both ways, Dr. T. I waited for five hours. What was I supposed to do for a hundred bucks an hour? Lie on a couch and talk to myself?

FOR THE EIGHTH STEP OF CHRISTMAS
MY SPONSOR GAVE TO ME
EIGHT POUNDS OF CHOCOLATE
SEVEN POUNDS OF CHOCOLATE
SIX POUNDS OF CHOCOLATE
FIVE POUNDS OF CHOCOLATE
FOUR POUNDS OF CHOCOLATE
THREE POUNDS OF CHOCOLATE
TWO POUNDS OF...

(She has a meltdown.) I ate it all! You...codependent enabler! You try breaking a board with you bare hand with nicotine patches all over your body! Yeah, I shopped, 'til I dropped! And your brother, Russell? *(Making an 'L' on her forehead.)* LOSER! And I still don't

have the serenity to find the courage to know the difference! Anyone got a match, I'm gonna smoke one of these friggin' patches!

(She starts to exit, dragging the mic stand behind her.)

OFFSTAGE VOICES.
AND A SESSION WITH HER THERAPIST,

WOMAN 2. *(Turning back to audience.)* Whatever!

OFFSTAGE VOICES.
TED!

(Blackout.)

PARTY SCENE

(Lights up on PIANO PLAYER looking at his book.)

BOOK. Give of Yourself this Holiday Season! Do you …. *(PIANO PLAYER turns page. Thinks. Turns page back.)* Give of Yourself this Holiday Season! Do you possess a special talent?
PIANO PLAYER. *(Realizing.)* Yes I do.
BOOK. … a special talent envied by others?
PIANO PLAYER. *(Affirming.)* Yes I do.
BOOK. … a talent that might bring joy to those around you?
PIANO PLAYER. *(Defiantly.)* Yes I do.
BOOK. Well, don't just sit there. Get up off that big Kris Kringle Kiester of yours…. Start sharing that talent. *(PIANO PLAYER stands.)* Start spreading that joy.
WOMAN 3. Start playing that piano, Santa Man—I'm paying you ten dollars and hour!
PIANO PLAYER. Twenty.

(PIANO PLAYER plays Christmas carol adagio.
Lights reveal up WOMAN 1 and MAN 2 standing just out of earshot.
Clearly they are having a terrible time and can't wait to leave the boredom and awkwardness of this party.)

WOMAN 3. *(To PIANO PLAYER, out of earshot of other*

couple.) Party's going well, don't you think?

PIANO PLAYER. *(Trying to remain polite, but with no enthusiasm.)* I'm having fun.

WOMAN 3. Have you tried the clam dip?

PIANO PLAYER. Yes, I have.

WOMAN 3. And ...?

PIANO PLAYER. Mmm ... oooh ....

WOMAN 3. Thank you.

MAN 2. *(Beyond earshot of WOMAN 3.)* All right, let's leave. She'll never miss us.

WOMAN 1. Honey, we're the only two people here!

MAN 2. I had more fun at your aunt Ellen's wake.

WOMAN 1. We were the only two people there, too.

MAN 2. But at that point, Aunt Ellen didn't care if we left. Speaking of Aunt Ellen, have you tried the clam dip?

WOMAN 1. I think it's seen better days.

WOMAN 3. I'm really glad I hired a piano player this year. You're really talented.

PIANO PLAYER. Thanks.

WOMAN 3. Music really makes a party.

MAN 2. I usually read the directions before I make something.

(WOMAN 1 and MAN 2 laugh. WOMAN 3 hears them from across room, thinking they're enjoying themselves, laughs too. They wave to each other across the room.)

WOMAN 3. *(To PIANO PLAYER.)* Everyone seems to be having such a good time. This is a much better party than last year.

MAN 2. *(To WOMAN 1 so WOMAN 3 can hear.)* Oh my, look at the time. We really must be going ....

WOMAN 1. *(Keeping him in the room and pushing him toward piano.)* ... over to the piano and sing some Christmas carols. *(To PIANO PLAYER.)* Do you know any of those ho, ho, ho, uh, ha, ha, ha, uh, hee, hee, hee, Christmas songs?

PIANO PLAYER. *(Taking off his hat and revealing a yarmulke.)* I'm Jewish.

WOMAN 1. Don't you watch TV? Everybody knows Frosty the 'Hoo Ha.'

MAN 2. Rudolf the nose boy.

WOMAN 3. The little drummer guy.

PIANO PLAYER. Why didn't you say so?

CHRISTMAS PARTY MEDLEY

PIANO PLAYER. *(Launching in enthusiastically.)*
HAVE A HOLLY JOLLY CHRISTMAS
IT'S THE BEST TIME OF THE YEAR.
    Add WOMAN 3. *(Thrilled.)*
I DON'T KNOW IF THERE'LL BE SNOW
BUT HAVE A CUP OF CHEER.

    Add WOMAN 1. *(Jumping in.)*
HAVE A HOLLY JOLLY CHRISTMAS,
AND WHEN YOU WALK DOWN THE STREET
SAY HELLO TO FRIENDS YOU KNOW
AND EV'RYONE YOU MEET.

(MAN 2 heads toward exit.)

    WOMEN.
OH, HO, THE MISTLETOE
HUNG WHERE YOU CAN SEE.
    MAN 2. *(Indicating the time on his watch.)*
SOMEBODY WAITS FOR YOU,
KISS HIM ONCE FOR ME.

(WOMAN 1 crosses to MAN 2, kisses him and pushes him back into the party. Trapped, MAN 2 launches into his own song.)

WOMEN.	**MAN 2.**
HAVE A HOLLY JOLLY CHRISTMAS	RUDOLPH,
AND IN CASE YOU DIDN'T HEAR	THE RED NOSED REINDEER, HAD A
OH, BY GOLLY	VERY SHINNY NOSE, AND IF YOU
HAVE A HOLLY JOLLY CHRISTMAS	EVER SAW IT YOU WOULD EVEN SAY IT
THIS YEAR	GLOWS

    WOMAN 1. *(Jumping on piano and "swingin" it.)*
FROSTY THE SNOWMAN
WAS A JOLLY HAPPY SOUL

WITH A CORN COB PIPE AND A BUTTON NOSE
AND TWO EYES MADE OUT OF COAL

(MAN 2 and WOMAN 3 playfully back her up.)

WOMAN 1.	**MAN 2 & WOMAN 3.**
DOWN TO THE VILLAGE	BAH-BUP BUP BAH ...
WITH A BROOMSTICK IN HIS HAND	OOO ...
RUNNING HERE AND THERE	BAH BAH DAH DUP BAH
AND AROUND THE SQUARE	DUM BI-YAH

ALL.
SAYIN', "CATCH ME IF YOU CAN!"

WOMAN 3. *(Running DS with her new idea.)* I know this one! *(She starts a child-like dance and the others join in.)*

PUT ONE FOOT IN FRONT OF THE OTHER
   WOMEN.
AND SOON YOU'LL BE WALKIN' CROSS THE FLOOR
   ALL.
PUT ONE FOOT IN FRONT OF THE OTHER
AND SOON YOU'LL BE WALKIN' OUT THE DOOR

YOU PUT ONE FOOT IN FRONT OF THE OTHER
AND SOON YOU'LL BE WALKIN' CROSS THE FLOOR
PUT ONE FOOT IN FRONT OF THE OTHER
AND SOON YOU'LL BE WALKIN' OUT ...

(Inhibitions gone, WOMAN 3 grabs MAN 2 and begins a "Salsa dance." He obliges, making WOMAN 1 jealous.)

WOMAN 3.
FELIZ NAVIDAD! FELIZ NAVIDAD!
FELIZ NAVIDAD! FELIZ NAVIDAD!
FELIZ NAVIDAD! FELIZ NAVIDAD!
FELIZ NAVIDAD! FELIZ NAVIDAD!

WOMAN 1. *(Putting the "Salsa" to an end.)* Hit me with a little Chipmunk in A-Flat.

CHRISTMAS, CHRISTMAS, CHRISTMAS IS HERE
TIME TO SING

(WOMAN 1 pulls MAN 2 away from WOMAN 3 by his ear.)

MAN 2.
DON'T PULL MY EAR
   ALL THREE.
PRESENTS WRAPPED WITH LOTS OF CARE
   MAN 2.
ME, I NEED NEW UNDERWEAR

(They give him a look.) What? I really do...

   ALL THREE.
WE ARE WAITING
ANTICIPATING
YES, WE'LL BE GOOD
   MAN 2.
I SWEAR ...
   WOMAN 3.
I'M ON THE ISLAND OF MISFIT TOYS
HERE I DON'T WANT TO STAY   **OTHERS.**
                                                    OOO...
   MAN 2.
I WANT TO TRAVEL WITH SANTA CLAUS
IN HER MAGIC SLEIGH

   WOMAN 3. *(Pulling him away with the "Salsa.")*
FELIZ NAVIDAD
   WOMAN 1.
FELIZ NAVIDAD
   BOTH.
FELIZ NAVIDAD

WOMAN 3.	**WOMAN 1.**
FELIZ NAVIDAD	PROSPEROS ANOS
FELIZ NAVIDAD	Y FLEICIDAD!

   WOMAN 1. *(Showing WOMAN 3 his ring.)*
SILVER AND GOLD, SILVER AND GOLD

A CHRISTMAS SURVIVAL GUIDE

EVERYONE WISHES FOR SILVER AND GOLD
HOW DO YOU MEASURE IT'S WORTH?
JUST BY THE PLEASURE IT GIVES HERE ON EARTH?

MAN 2.	**WOMEN.**
SILVER AND GOLD	
SILVER AND GOLD	SILVER AND GOLD
MEAN SO MUCH MORE WHEN I SEE	SILVER AND GOLD, I SEE
SILVER AND GOLD DECORATIONS	
ON EV'RY CHRISTMAS TREE	

(WOMAN 1 and MAN 2 are having a romantic, private moment.)

WOMAN 1.
CHESTNUTS ROASTING ON AN OPEN FIRE
JACK FROST NIPPING AT YOUR NOSE
  MAN 2.
YULETIDE CAROLS BEING SUNG BY A CHOIR
  WOMAN 1 & MAN 2.
AND FOLKS DRESSED UP LIKE ESKIMOS

(WOMAN 3 has gotten out her dust-buster and begins cleaning.

WOMAN 1 & MAN 2.	**WOMAN 3.**
EVERYBODY KNOW A TURKEY	*(Trying to jump in.)*
AND SOME MISTLETOE	FELIZ NAVIDAD
HELP TO MAKE THE SEASON BRIGHT	*(Offering dip between them.)* FELIZ NAVI-DIP?

(WOMAN 3 runs between them grabbing their hands.)

  WOMAN 3. *(Head in the air, to the tune of Hark the Herald …a la Charlie Brown Christmas.)*
LOO LOO LOO LOO LOO LOO LOO LOO
  ALL.
LOO LOO LOO LOO LOO LOO LOO
LOO LOO LOO LOO LOO LOO LOO LOO
LOO LOO LOO LOO LOO LOO LOO—

MAN 2. *(Looking at WOMAN 3.)*
FELIZ NAVIDAD
(Looking at WOMAN 1.)
FELIZ NAVIDAD
(Starting to dance with both.)
FELIZ NAVIDAD
PROSPERO ANOS Y FELIZIDAD

(It's a free-for-all. They're having the time of their lives.)

Add WOMEN.
FELIZ NAVIDAD
FELIZ NAVIDAD
FELIZ NAVIDAD
PROSPERO ANOS Y FELIZIDAD

I WANNA WISH YOU A MERRY CHRISTMAS
I WANNA WISH YOU A MERRY CHRISTMAS
I WANNA WISH YOU A MERRY CHRISTMAS
FROM THE BOTTOM OF MY HEART

I WANNA WISH YOU A MERRY CHRISTMAS
I WANNA WISH YOU A MERRY CHRISTMAS
I WANNA WISH YOU A MERRY CHRISTMAS
FROM THE BOTTOM OF MY HEART
FROM THE BOTTOM OF MY HEART

(The number buttons with everyone collapsing on the floor like children, laughing through the applause. WOMAN 1 and MAN 2 pick themselves up off the floor, giddy with delight. They ad lib as they leave the party about what a good time they've had. WOMAN 3 tries to keep them there, but to no avail. They say they can't wait 'til next year and exit, leaving WOMAN 3 to clean up. She takes her television remote and begins flipping through the channels. Lights flicker in a box patter center stage representing the glow from the television. She puts on a robe and fuzzy slippers and continues to clean as she flips through the various stations all playing well-known Christmas specials. Click.)

VOICEOVER or PRERECORDED. Don't change that channel! Next up on the Kid's Network, "Rudolph the Red Nosed Reindeer!"

(Click.) So gather your family around the television set and stay tuned for an Ozzy Osbourne Family Christmas Special, with special guest, Kathy Lee Gifford. *(Click.)* And that concludes this timeless holiday classic, where Clarence proves to us once again that it is indeed "A Wonderful Life"—and with the ring of a bell ... every angel does get his wings.

(SFX bells. Click. As the movie is now over, she feels more alone than ever. She sings.)

LITTLE GIRL BLUE

WOMAN 3.
SIT THERE AND COUNT YOUR FINGERS
WHAT CAN YOU DO
LITTLE GIRL, YOU'RE THROUGH
SIT THERE AND COUNT YOUR LITTLE FINGERS
UNHAPPY LITTLE GIRL BLUE

SIT THERE AND COUNT THE RAINDROPS
FALLING ON YOU
IT'S TIME YOU KNEW
ALL YOU CAN EVER COUNT ON
ARE THE RAINDROPS
THAT FALL ON LITTLE GIRL BLUE

NO USE OLD GIRL
YOU MAY AS WELL SURRENDER
YOUR HOPE IS GETTING SLENDER
WHY WON'T SOMEBODY SEND
A TENDER BLUE BOY
TO CHEER LITTLE GIRL BLUE

MEN AND WOMEN OFFSTAGE.
SILENT NIGHT, HOLY NIGHT
ALL IS CALM, ALL IS BRIGHT

WOMAN 3.
WHEN I WAS VERY YOUNG
THE WORLD WAS YOUNGER THAN I

NOW THE YOUNG WORLD HAS GROWN OLD
GONE ARE THE TINSEL AND GOLD.

SIT THERE AND COUNT THE RAINDROPS
FALLING ON YOU
IT'S TIME YOU KNEW
ALL YOU CAN EVER COUNT ON
ARE THE RAINDROPS THAT FALL ON
LITTLE GIRL BLUE

(Fade to black. WOMAN 3 exits.
WOMAN 2 is revealed downstage in light reading book, as Woman 3 and Man 1 prepare sleigh upstage.)

BOOK. Christmas is a time steeped in great tradition. Don't miss out. Gather with friends this holiday season and consider one of the following: singing Christmas carols around the fire, stringing cranberries and popcorn, making angels in the snow ....

AN OLD-FASHIONED SLEIGH RIDE

WOMAN 2. *(Closing book and moving into sleigh with other couple.)* A sleigh ride in the park. How festive.
ALL. *(Sitting together.)* Ahhh ....
WOMAN 3. ... it's so Currier and Ives.
MAN 1. I feel like Bing Crosby.
WOMAN 2. You look like Rosemary Clooney.
WOMAN 3. Honey, you ever drive a sleigh before?
MAN 1. Yeah, nothing to it. Just like driving a car.
WOMAN 2. One horse power.

(The very inventive PIANO PLAYER neighs as the sleigh takes off.)

WOMAN 3. Ooo, Rocky. Nice Horsy.
WOMAN 2. Rocky ... what a great name.
MAN 1. I wish I had a name like Rocky. It's so strong.
WOMAN 3. You just keep your eye on the road.

(This number is choreographed with the characters bouncing in their seats, miming each moment bump, turn and event along the way.)

ALL.
JUST HEAR THOSE SLEIGH BELLS JINGLING
RING - TING -TINGLING TOO
COME ON IT'S LOVELY WEATHER
FOR A SLEIGH RIDE TOGETHER WITH YOU
   MAN 1 & WOMAN 3.
OUTSIDE THE SNOW IS FALLING
AND FRIENDS ARE CALLING "YOO-HOO"
   WOMAN 2.
COME ON IT'S LOVELY WEATHER
   ALL.
FOR A SLEIGH RIDE TOGETHER WITH YOU

(They enjoy the bumps.)

   WOMAN 3.
GIDDY-UP
   MAN 1.
GIDDY-UP
   WOMAN 2.
GIDDY-UP
   ALL.
LET'S GO
LET'S LOOK AT THE SHOW.
WE'RE RIDING IN A WONDERLAND OF SNOW.
   WOMAN 2.
WE'RE RIDING ALONG WITH THE SNOW.

(They still enjoy the bumps.)

   WOMAN 3.
GIDDY-UP
   MAN 1.
GIDDY-UP
   WOMAN 2.
GIDDY-UP
   ALL.
IT'S GRAND
   WOMAN 3. *(Taking her boyfriend's hand.)*
JUST HOLDING YOUR HAND

(WOMAN 2 takes his other hand. He's starting to feel uncomfortable with all the attention.)

ALL.
WE'RE GLIDING ALONG WITH A SONG
OF A WINTRY FAIRYLAND

MAN 1. *(Breaking away from the handholds.)* Okay, ... which way do we go? Right or left?
WOMAN 2. How about the road less traveled, that's always fun.
WOMAN 3. I thought you said you knew what you were doing, honey.
MAN 1. I never said that, I just said that ....

(They all jerk to one side.)

WOMAN 3. Too late now, Rocky already decided.

ALL.
OUR CHEEKS ARE NICE AND ROSY
COMFY COZY ARE WEEE!
(Bump.)
WE'RE SNUGGLED UP TOGETHER
LIKE TWO BIRDS OF A FEATHER WOULD BE.

(Both WOMEN duck, MAN 1 is hit in the head by a tree branch.)

MAN 1. Oww!

ALL.
LET'S TAKE THAT ROAD BEFORE US
AND SING A CHORUS OR TWO.
COME ON, IT'S LOVELY WEATHER
FOR A SLEIGH RIDE TOGETHER WITH ...

WOMAN 3. Oh, no, Rocky's stuck in the mud!
MAN 1. *(Insert WOMAN 2's name)*, get out and push!
WOMAN 2. I'm in suede, you push!
MAN 1. I'm driving!
WOMAN 2. We've noticed.
WOMAN 3. Here, use this.

MAN 1. What is it?
WOMAN 2. A whip.
WOMAN 3. You know, just like at home.

(SFX of whip as horse neighs. The ACTORS yell and try to calm down the horse. They are now on a wild ride.)

ALL. *(Ad lib.)* Woo! Hey Rocky .... Nice horsy .... Whoa!!!!

JUST HEAR THOSE SLEIGH BELLS JINGLING
RING-TING-TINGLING TOO
COME ON IT'S LOVELY WEATHER
FOR A SLEIGH RIDE TOGETHER WITH YOU

OUTSIDE THE SNOW – FALL – FRIENDS – CALL

MAN 1. *(Standing.)* Get out of the way baldy!

ALL.
LOVELY WEATHER FOR A SLEIGH RIDE TOGETHER
   WOMAN 3.
OH MY GOD, OH MY GOD, OH MY GOD, WATCH OUT!
I THINK IT WAS A DOG.
   WOMAN 2 &MAN 1.
AWW!
   WOMAN 3.
I CAN'T TELL, I CAN'T SEE THROUGH THIS FOG
   ALL.
WOW!
   WOMAN 2.
OH MY GOD, OH MY GOD, A HOT DOG STAND!
   MAN 1.
YOU'RE HURTING MY HAND ...

WOMAN 3. *(To MAN 1.)* Sorry!	**WOMAN 2.** *(To imaginary hot dog vendor.)* Sorry!

ALL.
WE'RE RIDING ALONG PROVIDING THE GLIDING
AND THE SLIDING DOESN'T KILL US IN THIS
WET, COLD, WINTRY SCARY-LAND.

MAN 1.
THIS ISN'T WHAT I HAD PLANNED.

    WOMAN 2. You're going off the road!
    WOMAN 3. Turn!
    MAN 1. Too late!
    ALL. Ahh!

CHEEKS ROSY? COMFY? COZY? NO!
WE'RE HOLDING ON TOGETHER TO SEATS OF LEATHER

    WOMAN 2. And praying we don't fall out!

    ALL.
NO MORE ROAD BEFORE US
NOW THIS CHORUS IS THROUGH
COME ON, IT'S

(WOMEN are climbing on top of MAN 1.)

LOVELY WEATHER FOR A SLEIGH RIDE TOGETHER WITH
LOVELY WEATHER FOR A SLEIGH RIDE TOGETHER WITH
LOVELY WEATHER FOR A SLEIGH RIDE
LOVELY WEATHER FOR A SLEIGH RIDE
LOVELY WEATHER FOR A
LOVELY WEATHER FOR A
LOVELY WEATHER ...
AHH!

(Crash! Silence. Horse neigh. They open their eyes.)

    WOMAN 2. My pants. My suede pants ....
    MAN 1. Anybody seen my hat?

(WOMAN 2 takes his hat and forces it on his head covering his eyes.)

    WOMAN 3. That poor man in the wheelchair, I feel awful.

    ALL. *(Pulling themselves together and glad to be alive.)*
LOVELY WEATHER FOR A SLEIGH RIDE TOGETHER ...

    MAN 1. That was fun! Let's do it again!

A CHRISTMAS SURVIVAL GUIDE

(Horse neighs. Blackout.
CAROL OF THE BELLS music is heard. ALL enter the stage with a sense of optimism and accomplishment. They think they have discovered the meaning of Christmas …But through the course of the song, one-by-one they discover they haven't and exit discouraged, frustrated, and disappointed.)

BOOK. So how do you feel so far? By now, you should have acquired all the necessary tools to conquer each and every one of your holiday fears. The holiday spirit is yours for the taking.

EVERYBODY'S WAITIN' FOR THE MAN WITH THE BAG

ALL.
OLD MR. KRINGLE
IS SOON GONNA JINGLE
THE BELLS THAT'LL TINGLE ALL YOUR TROUBLES AWAY
EVERYBODY'S WAITIN' FOR THE MAN WITH THE BAG
'CUS CHRISTMAS IS HERE AGAIN

WOMAN 1.	**WOMEN 2 & 3.**	**MEN.**
OLD MR. KRINGLE IS SOON GONNA JINGLE THE BELLS *(Exits.)*	OLD MR. KRINGLE IS SOON GONNA JINGLE THE BELLS THAT'LL TINGLE ALL YOUR TROUBLES AWAY … YOUR TROUBLES AWAY …	
	EVERYBODY'S WAITIN' FOR THE MAN WITH THE BAG 'CUS CHRISTMAS *(Exits.)*	OLD MR. KRINGLE IS SOON GONNA JINGLE THE BELLS THAT'LL TINGLE ALL YOUR TROUBLES AWAY EVERYBODY'S WAITIN' FOR THE MAN WITH THE BAG 'CUS CHRISTMAS IS HERE … I SAID BRING ON THE CHEER … DON'T YOU KNOW CHRISTMAS IS HERE BRING ON THE CHEER

CHRISTMAS IS HERE
BRING ON THE CHEER
CHRISTMAS IS HERE
BRING ON THE CHEER ...

MAN 2. *(Tired of trying, he exits.)* Does anybody know the true meaning of Christmas???

PIANO PLAYER. Sure *(MAN 2's name here)*, I can tell you what Christmas is all about. Lights please.

(He crosses to center stage, stepping into a pool of light, and recites:)

RECITING OF CHRISTMAS STORY
(A la Linus from a Charlie Brown Christmas-Luke)

PIANO PLAYER. And, lo, the angel of the Lord came upon them, and the glory of the Lord shone round about them: and they were sore afraid. And the angel said unto them, Fear not: for, behold, I bring you good tidings of great joy, which shall be to all people. For unto you is born this day in the city of David a Savoir, which is Christ the Lord. And this shall be a sign unto you; Ye shall find the babe wrapped in swaddling clothes, lying in a manger. And suddenly there was with the angel a multitude of the heavenly host praising God, and saying, Glory to God in the highest, and on earth peace, good will toward men. And that's what Christmas is all about.

(PIANO PLAYER crosses back to piano as lights rise on singers.)

SACRED TRIO

WOMAN 2.
SOME CHILDREN SEE HIM LILY WHITE
THE BABY JESUS BORN THIS NIGHT
SOME CHILDREN SEE HIM LILY WHITE
WITH TRESSES SOFT AND FAIR

MAN 1.
SOME CHILDREN SEE HIM DARK AS THEY
SWEET MARY'S SON FOR WHOM WE PRAY
SOME CHILDREN SEE HIM DARK AS THEY

MAN 1 & WOMAN 2.
AND AH! THEY LOVE HIM TOO!
   WOMAN 1.
AWAY IN A MANGER, NO CRIB
   FOR HIS BED
THE LITTLE LORD JESUS LAY
   DOWN HIS SWEET HEAD
THE STARS IN THE HEAVENS
LOOKED DOWN WHERE HE LAY,
THE LITTLE LORD JESUS, ASLEEP
   IN THE HAY.
                                            WOMAN 2 & MAN 1.
                OOO…
THE CATTLE ARE LOWING, THE POOR BABY WAKES,
BUT LITTLE LORD JESUS NO CRYING HE MAKES

   WOMEN 1 & 2 & MAN 1.
AMAZING GRACE

WOMEN 1 & 2.	**WOMAN 3.**	**MAN 1.**
OO …	THE CHILDREN IN	OO …
AWAY IN A MANGER,	EACH DIFFERENT	AWAY IN A MANGER
NO CRIB FOR HIS BED	PLACE ...	NO CRIB FOR HIS BED
OO …	HMM … OOO ...	THEY'LL SEE THE
AMAZING GRACE	AMAZING GRACE	BABY JESUS FACE
HOW SWEET THE	HOW SWEET THE	LIKE THEIRS
SOUND	SOUND	HMM ...
I ONCE WAS LOST	I ONCE WAS LOST	I ONCE WAS LOST
BUT NOW I'M FOUND	BUT NOW I'M FOUND	BUT NOW I'M FOUND
	WAS BLIND	SOME CHILDREN SEE
AWAY IN A MANGER	BUT NOW I SEE	HIM ...

   ALL.
'TIS LOVE THAT'S BORN THIS NIGHT

(MAN 2 enters. He steps downstage center and sings.)

O HOLY NIGHT

   MAN 2.
O HOLY NIGHT

THE STARS ARE BRIGHTLY SHINING,
IT IS THE NIGHT
OF THE DEAR SAVIOR'S BIRTH.
LONG LAY THE WORLD
IN SIN AND ERROR PINING

TILL HE APPEARS
AND THE SOUL FELT IT'S WORTH.
A THRILL OF HOPE
THE WEARY WORLD REJOICES
FOR YONDER BREAKS
A NEW AND GLORIOUS MORN.

FALL ON YOUR KNEES!	**OTHERS.**
OH, HEAR THE ANGEL VOICES	OOO, OOO ...
O NIGHT DIVINE	
THE NIGHT WHEN CHRIST WAS BORN	

O NIGHT DIVINE
O NIGHT
O NIGHT DIVINE

FALL ON YOUR KNEES!
HEAR THE ANGEL VOICES
O NIGHT DIVINE
THE NIGHT WHEN CHRIST WAS BORN

O NIGHT DIVINE
O NIGHT DIVINE

(The lights fade on the SINGERS as they exit and music continues.)

BOOK. Year after year we watch "It's a Wonderful Life" thinking—that's it! That's the Christmas I want. I want to be George Bailey, hugging my family around the tree as friends and family throw money at us. But let's not forget, George Bailey lived life in his brother's shadow, abandoned his dreams to work for his father and nearly jumped off a bridge. Not exactly the hallmark life. Remember, the true magic of Christmas was not that he was about to jump, but that he didn't. And if you're still reading this book, you didn't jump either. So there you have it—you've been blessed by an angel just like

George. Never forget that. All you have left to do is hug your family under the tree and listen. Just listen. Not with your ears like an adult, but with your heart—like a child.

(One at a time, the SINGERS enter to sing. They each carry the book and now are looking at the world around them in a new way.)

THE GREATEST GIFT

WOMAN 3.
THE STREETS ARE BURSTING WITH A MILLION PEOPLE
THE STORES ARE FLASHING WITH A MILLION LIGHTS
AND WERE ALL SEARCHING FOR THAT SAME DREAM
THE GREATEST GIFT

MAN 1.
IT SEEMS THAT IF YOU HAD A MILLION DOLLARS
THAT YOU COULD MAKE A MILLION DREAMS COME TRUE
THEN YOU COULD BUY IT ALL AND GIVE WHAT COUNTS
THE GREATEST GIFT

WOMAN 2.
IN THE MIDST OF ALL THE FRANTIC RUSH
TAKE A BREATH AND YOU CAN FEEL YOUR HEART
 MAN 2.   **WOMAN 1.**
FEEL YOUR HEART   FEEL YOUR HEART

THERE'S A HUSH
 WOMAN 2.
THERE'S A HUSH   **WOMAN 3.**
            THERE'S

 ALL.
THE GREATEST GIFT, IS IN YOUR HEART
SO SHARE THE JOY, AND DO YOUR PART
REJOICE! AND LET LOVE START,
THE GIFT IS IN YOUR HEART

MAN 2.
EVRY YEAR THE SAME OLD MADNESS HAPPENS
 WOMAN 1.
SHOPPING LISTS THAT REACH A MILE LONG

WOMAN 3.
GOTTA BEAT THE CLOCK TO TRY AND FIND
THE GREATEST GIFT
    MEN.
JOY TO THE WORLD,
    WOMEN.
THE LORD IS COME
    MAN 1.
RACING ROUND THE TOWN WERE LOSING TRACK
    WOMAN 2.
OF WHAT IT MEANS TO REALLY CELEBRATE
    WOMAN 3.
YOU CAN GIVE WITHOUT A SINGLE DIME
    ALL.
THE GREATEST GIFT
    WOMAN 2 & MAN 1.
LET YOUR LOVE BE FOUND IN ALL YOU DO
    WOMAN 1.
SPREADING JOY TO PEOPLE
    ALL.
CLOSE TO YOU
CLOSE TO

THE GREATEST GIFT IS IN YOUR HEART
SO SHARE THE JOY AND DO YOUR PART
REJOICE! AND LET LOVE START
THE GIFT IS IN YOUR HEART

THE GREATEST GIFT
    MAN 1 & WOMAN 2.
GREATEST GIFT
    ALL.
IS IN YOUR HEART, SO SHARE THE JOY
    WOMAN 3 & MAN 2.
SHARE THE JOY
    ALL.
AND DO YOUR PART, REJOICE!

    WOMAN 1.
REJOICE

ALL.
AND LET LOVE START
THE GIFT IS IN YOUR HEART
AH! AH!
JOY TO THE WORLD, THE LORD IS COME
LET EARTH RECEIVE HER KING
LET EVERY HEART PREPARE HIM ROOM
AND HEAVEN AND NATURE SING
AND HEAVEN AND NATURE SING
AND HEAVEN, AND HEAVEN AND NATURE SING
HEAR IT SING

THE GREATEST GIFT IS IN YOUR HEART
SO SHARE THE JOY AND DO YOUR PART
REJOICE! AND LET LOVE START
THE GIFT IS IN YOUR HEART

THE GREATEST GIFT IS IN YOUR HEART
SO SHARE THE JOY AND DO YOUR PART
REJOICE! AND LET LOVE START
THE GIFT IS IN YOUR HEART
   WOMAN 1.
JOY TO THE WORLD
   MAN 1 & WOMAN 2.
THE GIFT IS IN YOUR HEART
   MAN 2.
JOY TO THE WORLD
   WOMAN 3.
THE GIFT IS IN YOUR HEART
   ALL.
AMEN

(Fade to black.)

BOWS: THE MAN WITH THE BAG

(Lights up. All are reading books. By end of voiceover, they realize they have been reading the same book.)

BOOK. Congratulations! You've made it. You have now acquired all the necessary tools to fully experience the wonder and magic of this holiday season, and holiday seasons yet to be! So what are you waiting for? Get out there! Join in those reindeer games! You'll soon discover what you've known all along—the true holiday spirit can't be found in a shopping mall or under a tree. It's been inside you all along—as plain as the nose on Rudolf's face.

ALL.
HE'LL MAKE THIS DECEMBER
THE ONE TO REMEMBER
THE BEST AND THE MERRIEST YOU EVER DID HAVE
EVERYBODY'S WAITIN'
    MAN 1.
EVERYBODY
    ALL.
THEY'RE ALL CONGREGATIN'
WAITIN' FOR THE MAN WITH THE BAG
    WOMAN 1.
WITH THE BAG
    OTHERS.
WITH THE BAG
    ALL.
YOU BETTER WATCH OUT NOW!
HO HO HO!

(All throw books in the air. Blackout.
Lights up. Bows.
ALL exit.)

THE END

APPENDIX A: MUSICAL NUMBERS FOR CAST OF 3

ACT I

Carol of the Bells	ALL
Everybody's Waitin' for the Man with the Bag	ALL
We Wish You a Merry Christmas	ALL
All Those Christmas Clichés	WOMAN 2
Silver Bells	MAN
The Christmas Party / I'd Like to Hitch a Ride with Santa Claus	WOMAN 1
The Happy New Year Blues	ALL
Reindeer Boogie / Jingle Bells	PIANO PLAYER, ALL
Christmas Eve	WOMAN 1
Santa Fantasy	MAN
Silent Night	INSTRUMENTAL
Surabaya Santa	WOMAN 2
Santa Claus Is Back in Town	ALL

ACT II

The Twelve Steps of Christmas	WOMAN 2
TV Christmas Medley	ALL
Rudolph the Red Nosed Reindeer	
A Holly Jolly Christmas	
Silver and Gold	
Frosty the Snowman	
Put One Foot in Front of the Other	
Feliz Navidad	
The Christmas Song	
Hark the Herald Angels Sing	
Little Girl Blue	WOMAN 1
An Old-Fashioned Sleigh Ride	ALL
Sacred Trio	ALL
Away in a Manger	
Some Children See Him	
Amazing Grace	
O Holy Night	ALL
The Greatest Gift	ALL
Everybody's Waitin' for the Man with the Bag	ALL

APPENDIX B: CHANGES FOR SMALLER CAST

The following adjustments are made to reduce the cast to 3.

ACT I

CAROL OF THE BELLS

WOMAN 2.
HARK, HOW THE BELLS
SWEET SILVER BELLS
ALL SEEM TO SAY
"THROW CARES AWAY"

VOICEOVER. Only 127 shopping days left.

WOMAN 2 & MAN.
CHRISTMAS IS HERE
BRINGING GOOD CHEER
TO YOUNG AND OLD
MEEK AND THE BOLD

VOICEOVER. Only 93 shopping days left!

ALL.
DING, DONG, DING, DONG
THAT IS THEIR SONG
WITH JOYFUL RING
ALL CAROLING

VOICEOVER. 73 days left!

WOMEN.
ONE SEEMS TO HEAR
WORDS OF GOOD CHEER
FROM EVERY WHERE
FILLING THE AIR

MAN.
DING DONG IN
FORTY-TWO MORE DAYS
VOICEOVER. 42 days.

MAN & WOMAN 2.
O, HOW THEY POUND
RAISING THE SOUND
O'ER HILL AND DALE
TELLING THEIR TALE

WOMAN 1.
DING DONG IN
THIRTY-THREE MORE DAYS.
VOICEOVER. Thirty-three.

MAN & WOMAN 1.
GAILY THEY RING
WHILE PEOPLE SING
WORDS OF GOOD CHEER
CHRISTMAS IS HERE!

WOMAN 2.
TWENTY-SEVEN MORE DAYS.
VOICEOVER. Twenty-seven.

WOMEN.
MERRY MERRY MERRY
CHRISTMAS

MAN.
IN FIVE DAYS
VOICEOVER. Five!

MAN & WOMAN 1.
MERRY MERRY MERRY
MERRY CHRISTMAS

WOMAN 2.
FOUR DAYS
VOICEOVER. Four!

MAN & WOMAN 2.
MERRY MERRY MERRY MERRY
MERRY MERRY
ALL.
CHRISTMAS IS HERE!
CHRISTMAS IS HERE!
CHRISTMAS IS HERE!
CHRISTMAS IS …

WOMAN 1.
THREE DAYS
VOICEOVER. Three!

VOICEOVER. Happy Thanksgiving!

THE MAN WITH THE BAG

WOMAN 2.
OLD MR. KRINGLE
IS SOON GONNA JINGLE
THE BELLS THAT'LL TINGLE ALL YOUR TROUBLES AWAY
EVERYBODY'S WAITIN' FOR THE MAN WITH THE BAG
'CAUSE CHRISTMAS IS COMIN' AGAIN

MAN.
HE'S GOT A SLEIGH FULL
IT'S NOT GONNA STAY FULL
WOMAN 1.
HE'S GOT STUFF TO DROP AT EVERY STOP OF THE WAY
MAN AND WOMAN 1.
EVERYBODY'S WAITIN' FOR THE MAN WITH THE BAG
ALL.
'CAUSE CHRISTMAS IS COMIN' AGAIN

WOMAN 2.
HE'LL BE HERE
WITH THE ANSWERS TO THE PRAYERS
THAT YOU'VE MADE THROUGH THE YEAR
WOMAN 1.
YOU'LL GET YOURS
IF YOU'VE DONE EVERYTHING YOU SHOULD
MAN.
BEEN EXTRA SPECIAL GOOD
WOMAN 1.
HE'LL MAKE THIS DECEMBER
WOMEN.
THE ONE YOU'LL REMEMBER
ALL.
THE BEST AND THE MERRIEST YOU EVER DID HAVE
EVERYBODY'S WAITIN' FOR THE MAN WITH THE BAG
CHRISTMAS IS HERE AGAIN

ALL. *(During voiceover.)*
FA, LA LA LA. FA, LA LA LA …
FA LA LA, HAPPY HOLIDAY!

OLD MR. KRINGLE
IS SOON GONNA JINGLE
ALL THE BELLS THAT'LL TINGLE ALL YOUR TROUBLES AWAY
EVERYBODY'S WAITIN' FOR THE MAN WITH THE BAG
CHRISTMAS IS HERE AGAIN

WOMAN 1.
HE'LL BE HERE
WITH THE ANSWER TO
 THE PRAYERS
THAT YOU'VE MADE THROUGH
 THE YEAR
MAN.
YOU'LL GET YOURS

IF YOU'VE DONE EVERYTHING
 YOU SHOULD

WOMAN 2.
BEEN EXTRA SPECIAL GOOD
WOMAN 1.
JUST LIKE I KNEW YOU WOULD

ALL.
HE'LL MAKE THIS DECEMBER
THE ONE TO REMEMBER
THE BEST AND THE MERRIEST
 YOU EVER DID HAVE
WOMEN.
EVERYBODY'S WAITIN'
ALL.
THEY'RE ALL CONGREGATIN'
WAITIN' FOR THE MAN
WOMAN 1.
WITH THE BAG

ALL.
YOU BETTER WATCH OUT NOW!

WOMAN 2 & MAN.
HE'LL BE HERE

WOMEN.
YOU'LL GET YOURS

MAN.
EVERYBODY

WOMAN 2 & MAN.
WITH THE BAG

WE WISH YOU A MERRY CHRISTMAS

ALL.
WE WISH YOU A MERRY CHRISTMAS
WE WISH YOU A MERRY CHRISTMAS
WE WISH YOU A MERRY CHRISTMAS
AND A HAPPY NEW YEAR.

WOMAN 2.
WE WISH YOU A MERRY CHRISTMAS
AND A HAPPY NEW YEAR

MAN & WOMAN 1.
BA DA BA DA ...

A CHRISTMAS SURVIVAL GUIDE

ALL THOSE CHRISTMAS CLICHÉS – WOMAN 2

SILVER BELLS – MAN

CUT *THIS WILL BE THE BEST CHRISTMAS EVER*

THE CHRISTMAS PARTY/I'D LIKE TO HITCH A RIDE WITH SANTA CLAUS – WOMAN 1

(At then end of the playoff, WOMAN 2 joins her.)

THE HAPPY NEW YEAR BLUES

WOMAN 2.
OUT IN THE STREET
HEAR THE BEAT OF A DRUM
IT'S TWELVE O'CLOCK AND THE NEW YEAR HAS COME
JUST HEAR THEM YELL
AS THEY WELCOME THE NEWS
I SHOULD BE GLAD BUT I'M NOT
'CUS I'M SAD 'CUS
I'VE GOT THE HAPPY NEW YEAR BLUES

THE VERY FIRST OF EACH JANUARY
KEEPS GETTING WORSE
'CUS I HAVE TO CARRY
ONE MORE YEAR
WITH NOBODY NEAR
WHO FEELS JUST THE SAME AS I

(MAN enters.)

    MAN. *(Reading back cover of book.)* Other Books by Author: "Searching for Your Soul Mate," "Finding that Special Romance," "Embracing Your Dog."
    PIANO PLAYER. Embracing your …?
    MAN. Don't knock it till you've tried it, married man.

OUT IN THE STREET THE CROWD WALKING
SHOUTING A HIP HURRAY
FILLING THE NIGHT WITH LOVE, WALKING
I SEEM TO HEAR THEM SAY
HERE COMES OLD FATHER TIME
BRINGING PLENTY OF HAPPY NEWS
EVERYONE'S GLAD WHILE I'M SINGING
THE HAPPY NEW YEAR BLUES

(WOMAN 1 enters reading book.)

    WOMAN 1. It's impossible to meet anyone during the holidays. Everyone's so happy and gay or happy *and* gay!
    PIANO PLAYER. Not that there's anything wrong with that.
    WOMAN 1. Easy for you to say, married man.

WOMAN 1.
A WEDDING RING
A SWEET BRIDAL BOUQUET
AND EVERYTHING I KNOW WOULD BE OK
BUT EACH DAY IT'S FURTHER AWAY
AND MY HOW THE TIME DOES FLY

COUNTING THE DAYS UNTIL
SOMEONE GIVES ME SOME SYMPATHY
HOPING TO GET A THRILL
FROM ONE WHO'LL GET A THRILL FROM ME

ALL.
YEAR AFTER YEAR I GROW OLDER
SOON THEY WILL ALL BE GONE
GOING THROUGH LIFE WITH NO SHOULDER
TO LAY MY HEAD UPON

PIANO PLAYER. Perhaps a slight adjustment in your attitudes would ...
ALL. Shut up, Married man.

BRING OUT THE OLD YEAR AND RING IN THE NEW
MEANS NOTHING TO SOMEONE WHO FEELS SO BLUE
THERE GOES MY PHONE
BUT IT'S NOT HAPPY NEWS
CENTRAL IS RINGING MY PHONE JUST TO WISH ME
A HAPPY NEW YEAR BLUES
A VERY HAPPY NEW YEAR BLUES

(Blackout.)

REINDEER BOOGIE & JINGLE BELLS – **PIANO PLAYER**

CHRISTMAS EVE - **WOMAN 2**

(A lighting special appears on the floor in the shape of a square, representing an elevator. Whenever someone pushes the elevator button, the piano player plays a note on the piano. WOMAN 1 enters and crosses to elevator door carrying packages, she pushes the button. MAN enters carrying a large shopping bag. In a rush, he hits the button three times. Ignoring each other and turning front, they read the book.

BOOK. According to a recent poll of holiday shoppers, the second greatest fear during "The Season of Giving" is balancing one's checkbook!

(Sound effect: ding, elevator doors open.
The two step in the elevator. They each push a button. As the doors are about to shut, WOMAN 2 rushes on and to the elevator. Using her purse to stop the door, it reopens. She steps in with the others. She pushes a button but it's the wrong one so she pushes another, irritating the others. The doors shut. The elevator musak begins. They all pull out their books and read.)

A CHRISTMAS SURVIVAL GUIDE

IT'S BEGINNING TO LOOK A LOT LIKE CHRISTMAS
(Musical Underscoring — Prerecorded)

BOOK. ... The first greatest fear of the holiday season, surprisingly enough, is *not* getting invited to Christmas parties.
Sound Effect: Elevator DING!
FEMALE VOICEOVER. Third floor—Auto Parts, Garden Equipment, Ladies' Lingerie.

(Doors open, WOMAN 1 exits elevator. Doors close. Musak.)

BOOK. Combine these two issues, and it's enough to bring even George Baily to the bridge.

(Sound effect: elevator DING! As MAN 2 chuckles, WOMAN 2 catches him. They smile at each other for a moment.)

FEMALE VOICEOVER. Seventh floor—Home Electronics, Office Furniture, Ladies' Lingerie.

(Doors open, WOMAN 2 exits. The doors close. Musak.)

BOOK. Well here's a way to kill two turtledoves with one stone. Not only is it a great way to sock away some extra cash, it's also guaranteed to be an exciting and fun way to meet new and interesting people: Seasonal Employment.

(Sound effect: elevator DING!)

FEMALE VOICEOVER. Tenth floor—Customer Service, Santa's Village!
MAN 2. Ladies' Lingerie.
FEMALE VOICEOVER. ... and of course, Ladies' Lingerie.

(Sound effect: doors open. MAN exits elevator.)

BOOK. Seasonal employment can take many forms ....

(Sound effect: elevator doors close. MUSIC BEGINS.)

SANTA FANTASY – MAN

SKETCH OF SANTA'S VILLAGE – WOMAN 2

SURABAYA SANTA – WOMAN 1

SANTA CLAUS IS BACK IN TOWN – MAN

(Cut crossover at end of number.)

ACT II

THE TWELVE STEPS OF CHRISTMAS – WOMAN 2

PARTY SCENE

(WOMAN 1 is having the party; WOMAN 2 and MAN are the guests.)

LITTLE GIRL BLUE – WOMAN 1

AN OLD-FASHIONED SLEIGH RIDE

(WOMAN 1 reads WOMAN 3)

EVERYBODY'S WAITIN' FOR THE MAN WITH THE BAG

(Delete WOMAN 3.)

SACRED TRIO

WOMAN 1.
SOME CHILDREN SEE HIM LILY WHITE
THE BABY JESUS BORN THIS NIGHT
SOME CHILDREN SEE HIM LILY WHITE
WITH TRESSES SOFT AND FAIR

MAN.
SOME CHILDREN SEE HIM DARK AS THEY
SWEET MARY'S SON FOR WHOM THEY PRAY
SOME CHILDREN SEE HIM DARK AS THEY
    MAN & WOMAN 1.
AND AH! THEY LOVE HIM TOO!

WOMAN 2
AWAY IN A MANGER, NO CRIB FOR HIS BED
THE LITTLE LORD JESUS LAY DOWN HIS SWEET HEAD
THE STARS IN THE HEAVENS
LOOKED DOWN WHERE HE LAY,
THE LITTLE LORD JESUS, ASLEEP IN THE HAY.
THE CATTLE ARE LOWING, THE POOR BABY WAKES,
BUT LITTLE LORD JESUS NO CRYING HE MAKES

    ALL.
AMAZING GRACE

WOMEN 2.	**WOMAN 1.**	**MAN 1.**
OO …	THE CHILDREN IN EACH DIFFERENT PLACE …	OO …
AWAY IN A MANGER, NO CRIB FOR HIS BED		AWAY IN A MANGER NO CRIB FOR HIS BED
OO …	HMM … OOO … AMAZING GRACE …	THEY'LL SEE THE BABY

A CHRISTMAS SURVIVAL GUIDE

AMAZING GRACE	HOW SWEET THE SOUND	JESUS FACE
HOW SWEET THE SOUND	I ONCE WAS LOST	LIKE THEIRS
I ONCE WAS LOST	BUT NOW I'M FOUND	HMM ...
BUT NOW I'M FOUND	WAS BLIND	I ONCE WAS LOST
	BUT NOW I SEE	BUT NOW I'M FOUND
AWAY IN A MANGER		SOME CHILDREN SEE HIM

    ALL.
'TIS LOVE THAT'S BORN THIS NIGHT

(MAN enters. He steps downstage center and sings.)

O HOLY NIGHT - MAN

THE GREATEST GIFT

    WOMAN 2.
THE STREETS ARE BURSTING WITH A MILLION PEOPLE
THE STORES ARE FLASHING WITH A MILLION LIGHTS
AND WERE ALL SEARCHING FOR THAT SAME DREAM
THE GREATEST GIFT
    MAN.
IT SEEMS THAT IF YOU HAD A MILLION DOLLARS
THAT YOU COULD MAKE A MILLION DREAMS COME TRUE
THEN YOU COULD BUY IT ALL AND GIVE WHAT COUNTS
THE GREATEST GIFT
    WOMAN 1.
IN THE MIDST OF ALL THE FRANTIC RUSH
TAKE A BREATH AND YOU CAN FEEL YOUR HEART

MAN.	**WOMAN 2.**
FEEL YOUR HEART	FEEL YOUR HEART
THERE'S A HUSH	
THERE'S A HUSH	
	THERE'S A HUSH

    ALL.
THE GREATEST GIFT, IS IN YOUR HEART
SO SHARE THE JOY, AND DO YOUR PART
REJOICE! AND LET LOVE START, THE GIFT IS IN YOUR HEART

    MAN.
EVRY YEAR THE SAME OLD MADNESS HAPPENS
    WOMAN 1.
SHOPPING LISTS THAT REACH A MILE LONG

WOMAN 2.
GOTTA BEAT THE CLOCK TO TRY AND FIND
THE GREATEST GIFT
    MAN.
JOY TO THE WORLD,
    WOMAN 1.
 THE LORD IS COME
    MAN.
RACING ROUND THE TOWN WERE LOSING TRACK
    WOMAN 1.
OF WHAT IT MEANS TO REALLY CELEBRATE
    WOMAN 2.
YOU CAN GIVE WITHOUT A SINGLE DIME
    ALL.
THE GREATEST GIFT
    WOMAN 2 & MAN.
LET YOUR LOVE BE FOUND IN ALL YOU DO
    WOMAN 1.
SPREADING JOY TO PEOPLE
    ALL.
CLOSE TO YOU CLOSE TO YOU

THE GREATEST GIFT IS IN YOUR HEART
SO SHARE THE JOY AND DO YOUR PART
REJOICE! AND LET LOVE START
THE GIFT IS IN YOUR HEART

THE GREATEST GIFT
    MAN.
GREATEST GIFT
    ALL.
IS IN YOUR HEART, SO SHARE THE JOY
    WOMAN 2.
SHARE THE JOY

    ALL.
AND DO YOUR PART, REJOICE!

    WOMAN 1.
REJOICE
    ALL.
AND LET LOVE START
THE GIFT IS IN YOUR HEART

AH! AH!
JOY TO THE WORLD, THE LORD IS COME
LET EARTH RECEIVE HER KING
LET EVERY HEART PREPARE HIM ROOM
AND HEAVEN AND NATURE SING
AND HEAVEN AND NATURE SING
AND HEAVEN, AND HEAVEN AND NATURE SING
HEAR IT SING

THE GREATEST GIFT IS IN YOUR HEART
SO SHARE THE JOY AND DO YOUR PART
REJOICE! AND LET LOVE START
THE GIFT IS IN YOUR HEART

THE GREATEST GIFT IS IN YOUR HEART
SO SHARE THE JOY AND DO YOUR PART
REJOICE! AND LET LOVE START
THE GIFT IS IN YOUR HEART

 WOMAN 1.
JOY TO THE WORLD
 MAN & WOMAN 2.
THE GIFT IS IN YOUR HEART
 MAN.
JOY TO THE WORLD
 WOMAN 2.
THE GIFT IS IN YOUR HEART
 ALL.
AMEN

PROPS

3 guide books
Cell phone
Telephone
Tray with clam dip
Mic stand with prop mic
Salvation Army bell
Red bucket
Coffee cup
Puppet (in shopping bag)
Candy Cane
Pad and pen
Suitcase
String of lights
Dustbuster

COSTUMES

Garland boa
Santa suit for women: hat, coat, pants, beard and mustache
4 reindeer antlers
Leopard scarf and handbag
Dark sunglasses
Black gloves
Jewel-tone scarf
Full men's Santa suit: hat, pants, spats, coat, beard and mustache
Bing Crosby hat
Angel hat
Flap hat
Rudolph nose
Santa hat
Yarmulke
TV remote

A CHRISTMAS SURVIVAL GUIDE

SET DESIGN

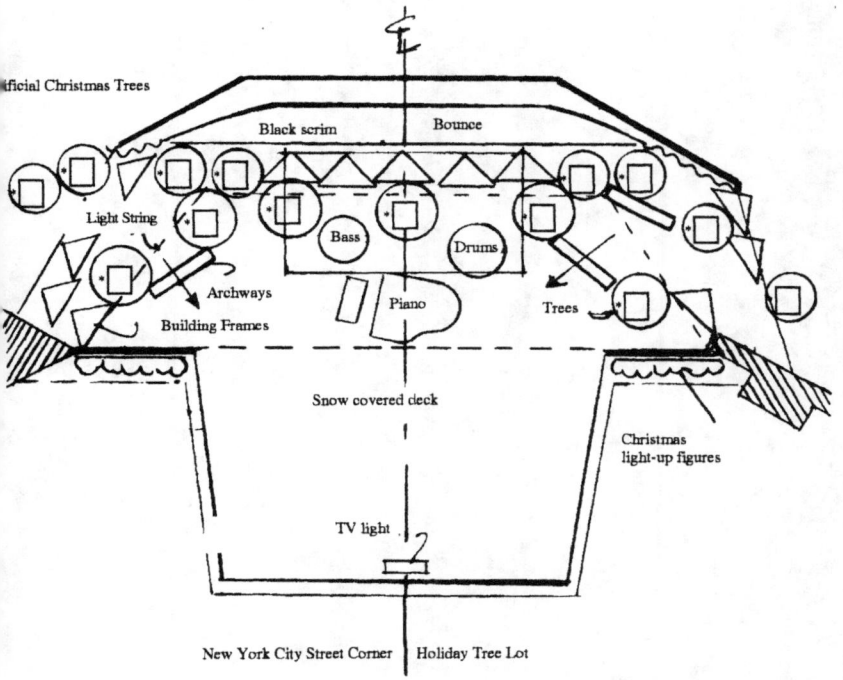

Designed by Dana L. Kenn

www.ingramcontent.com/pod-product-compliance
Lightning Source LLC
Chambersburg PA
CBHW072018290426
44109CB00018B/2277